D1738798

Take It
to the
Limit

Take It to the Limit

Julie Ridge
and
Judith Zimmer

Rawson Associates : New York

Library of Congress Cataloging in Publication Data

Ridge, Julie.
  Take it to the limit.

  Bibliography: p. 194
  Includes index.
  1. Sports—Psychological aspects. 2. Mind and body.
3. Achievement motivation. I. Zimmer, Judith, II. Title.
GV706.4.R53 1986   796'.01   84-42934
ISBN 0-89256-281-1

Copyright © 1986 by Julie Ridge, Judith Zimmer, and
The Miller Press
All rights reserved
Published simultaneously in Canada by
Collier Macmillan Canada, Inc.
Packaged by Rapid Transcript, a division of March Tenth, Inc.
Composition by Folio Graphics Co., Inc.
Manufactured by Fairfield Graphics, Fairfield, Pennsylvania
Designed by Jacques Chazaud
First Edition

This book is not intended as a substitute for medical advice of physicians. The reader should regularly consult a physician in matters relating to his or her health and particularly in respect of any symptoms which may require diagnosis or medical attention.

To my most valuable and trusted friends—
my mom, dad, and sisters Lisa and Susan
—J. R.

To Louis, Natalie, and Donald Zimmer
—J. Z.

Contents

ACKNOWLEDGMENTS   *xi*

WHAT'S IT ALL ABOUT?   *3*

Part I The Mind   *11*

1 "I Did It!"   *13*
2 Training: The Mental Process   *23*
3 The Techniques That Develop Mental Toughness   *38*
4 Knowing How Far Is Too Far: Avoiding Burnout   *52*
5 The Finishing Syndrome   *63*
6 Not Finishing: Learning from It
     and Living with It   *80*
7 After Success/Post-Event Depression   *92*

Part II The Body   *101*

8 The High-Energy Endurance Life-Style   *103*

ix

9   Finding the Marathon in You   *112*

10   How the Ultras Train to Finish   *125*

11   Journey Through the Body   *136*

12   Journey Through Bodily Pain   *158*

13   Common Questions and Unorthodox Answers About Endurance Sports   *179*

BIBLIOGRAPHY AND SUGGESTED READING   *194*

INDEX   *197*

Acknowledgments

Vicky Aden, Paul Asmuth, George L. Ball, Lyn Brooks, Peter Costiglio, Chris Files, Mike Frankfurt, Sally Friedman, David Gibbons, Dr. Doug Hiller, Berenice Hoffman, John Howard, Dr. Andrew Jacobs, P. J. Johnson, Rebecca Kelly, Jeremy Larner, John LeGear, Jenifer Levin, Steven Lichtman, Tracy Lynn, Angela Miller, Stu Mittleman, Cindy Nicholas, Bev Norwood, Mary O'Toole, Eleanor and Kennett Rawson, Bob Reese, Bill Schmidt, Saul Schoenberg, Toni Sciarra, Dan Sikowitz, Laurie Solomon, Spike Steingasser, Gail Stentiford, Dr. Murray Weisenfeld, Jody Weiss

Take It to the Limit

What's It All About?

Every generation has its own adventurers, its dare-devils. Today's adventurers are doing the same sports as everyone else—running, swimming, and bicycling—except that they're pushing themselves to the limit. The challenge for the endurance athlete comes from within: It's you against yourself. You test your own limits. Nothing comes between you and your goal but the body and mind—both of which must be trained to finish.

It's not only athletes who incorporate endurance into their lives. There are all sorts of people—doctors, lawyers, parents, businesspeople, students, artists—who also push themselves to the limit. Anytime you challenge yourself and achieve something; anytime you set a goal, go after it, and reach it, you are pushing yourself. You make endurance part of your life when you put out your greatest effort and do your best.

I am an endurance athlete. In September 1982 I swam the English Channel. The next summer, July 1983, I became the first person to swim two consecutive laps around Manhattan. The following year I completed the Hawaii Ironman triathlon, a combined 2.4-mile swim, 112-mile bike ride, and 26.2 mile run. I may not be fast, but I can last a very long time. I had to experiment to find that out. Pushing back the limits of endurance became as satisfying for me as winning the gold is to the Olympian.

Any one of us can do more than we think we can. I know because I wasn't always an endurance athlete. I was an actress working on Broadway, who, like most people, wanted to realize—and work toward—my potential. Swimming became my medium. The impossible became possible. Who would have thought that just one year after swimming two miles for the first time, I could swim for eighteen hours across the English Channel?

What gives an individual the power to endure? Where does the drive come from? Endurance comes from strength, willpower, sheer desire, raw courage, and—sometimes—loneliness. "Why do you do it?" I am asked over and over again. "Why not?" I usually reply. But there is more to it. *Everyone has untapped potential.* It's often easier to be lazy than to push ourselves and see what we can do. Endurance gave me the chance to see what I've got, and it can do the same for you.

Why Endure?

Endurance is part of everyone's life—whether it's in the gym, at the office, or at home. You are experiencing the phenomenon of endurance whenever you:

4

- *Test your limits* by staying up all night to prepare a presentation or finish a term paper
- *See how far you can go* by running farther than you've ever run before—whether it's three miles or three hundred
- *Do more* by joining a new company and immediately picking up two new clients
- *Take on a challenge* by raising two children and holding down a job
- *Work toward a goal* by trying to increase your firm's revenue by 50 percent in a year
- *Push yourself* by starting your own company

Whenever you test your limits or strive toward a goal, you are taking control and *accepting responsibility for your own life.* To the endurance athlete, setting a goal and going after it is a natural, welcome challenge. Endurance tests the body, soul, and mind because it is difficult, raw, and burdensome. It has its rewards, though. Putting out that effort gives you a powerful sense of satisfaction. Enduring is magical, alluring, and addicting. It is a celebration of your own life, your ability, and your potential.

Endurance Brings Good Things to Life

Living life intensely and devoting yourself to a passion—in any field—is life-affirming. Putting out that extra effort brings good things to all aspects of your life.

Stu Mittleman, an ultra-distance runner who won the hundred-mile National Championship in 1980, 1981, and 1982 and who has also been a professor of sports psychology and sociology, explains that he lives the way he feels comfortable living. "That's with an intensity. I do it day to

5

day. I get up in the morning and think, 'What can I do today? What can I accomplish?' "

Ask yourself the same questions. *What can I do today? What can I accomplish?* If you feel as though you are in a rut, if you feel unmotivated or unchallenged, examine your circumstances. If the following attitudes apply to you, you are probably just existing, not pushing yourself.

- Lack of interest in your project
- Dependency on other people to make decisions that affect your life
- Insecurity about your abilities, talents, and skills
- Self-defeating feelings which keep you from trying
- Passivity about your goals and future

Goals must be individually chosen. Establish what yours are. One person's marathon is one hundred miles, another person's five miles. One person's goal may be getting a new job; another person's, getting elected to the State Senate. Only you know the direction in which you want your life to go.

To assess your goals, ask yourself the following questions:

- What are my strong points or talents?
- What subjects am I interested in and concerned about?
- How can I connect what I am interested in with my strong points?

Take direction from the answers to these questions. They might not lead directly to a viable goal, but they will help guide you.

Integrating fitness or sports into your life is *one* way of upgrading your life-style and infusing your body with energy. Says ultra-distance cyclist and 1981 Hawaii Ironman winner John Howard, "I think people are looking for something to improve themselves, and sports are a way of finding that. We're not as content to sit home on Sunday with a six-pack of beer and watch other gladiators battle it out. We want to be out there doing something for ourselves."

People *are* out there "doing something for themselves"—whether their passion is sports, business, or the arts. And they are discovering—as you will—that the benefits of endurance dramatically alter their lives.

Getting Endurance into Your Life

Take It to the Limit is about preparing the mind and the body to endure. We will show you what endurance means and what it takes to push yourself in the era of endurance.

We will present the phenomenon of endurance in its purest form by examining the lives of athletes who deliberately and intelligently spend the central hours of every day preparing for an endurance challenge. These ultra-athletes perform endurance activities that involve constant, monotonous movement lasting more than four or five hours and sometimes for several days in succession. Some have swum across the English Channel, run six-day races, bicycled nearly 3,000 miles in less than ten days in the Race Across AMerica, or participated in an Ironman triathlon.

We'll also show you how people from all walks of life have made endurance part of their lives—and how you can, too. *You'll find out what you have in common with people who push back their limits and how you can go farther and do more in your own life.* You *can* do things you've never tried before. *There is a marathon in everyone.*

7

The Mental Mile

Mental strength is behind all endurance efforts. Even ultra-athletes need more than physical strength to get through an event. They need mental endurance, strength of will, and imagination to plan their training, follow it through, and be in command of their chosen event.

In the first part of this book we'll explain what mental endurance is and how *your* mind can be trained to help you push back your limits. There is a powerful store of motivation and determination behind any effort and a wonderful feeling of elation that accompanies pushing back your limits, whether you're running five miles for the first time or making your first sale. These positive feelings can inspire a drive toward greater and greater challenges.

You'll learn how to map out a program for getting to your goal and how people endure the toughest spots of the whole process—those times when they want more than anything in the world to quit. What's the key to holding your course and not giving up when the going gets tough?

We'll show you how to tell if you're pushing yourself too hard or too fast, how to avoid burnout, and how to harness your energy so that it works *for* you, not against you. The event itself—be it a swim across Lake Ontario or an urgent deadline—warrants a great deal of mental and emotional energy, often creating a severe letdown when it's over. How do you cope with postevent depression?

You won't succeed every time. But you should be able to make every experience count, whether it is successful or not. Let your failures and mistakes instruct you.

What's It All About?

Taking Your Body to
the Limit

The second part of *Take It to the Limit* analyzes the physical aspects of enduring. Have you ever wanted to ask highly accomplished, active individuals how they do it? Where do they get their energy? We've explored where human energy comes from and encapsulated the clues to living a high-energy endurance life-style.

There are also guidelines for finding the marathon in you, suggestions for beginning a fitness program if you don't already have one, and safe ways to increase your endurance for a healthier life-style. However, this book is not an athlete's training manual. Each ultra-athlete has developed his or her individual training program; there is no single training regime that works for everyone. These are athletes who have listened to their own bodies and devised their own training programs. If your endurance efforts involve athletics, we recommend that you experiment with workout schedules until you find what feels right for you—and, of course, that you consult with your physician before beginning any fitness program.

When you respect your body and treat it well—when you take it out for a walk or a swim or run—it will smile and tingle all day. All it requires is taking responsibility for your well-being. Develop and enjoy your own strength and power. You'll respect yourself more for the extra effort.

To show you the physical effects of endurance, we'll take you on a journey through a healthy exercising body. In this way you can understand what's happening inside your body while you exercise and how endurance affects human energy and lifelong health.

A journey through bodily pain will allow you to understand and cope with discomfort while you're working out.

We'll explain how injuries occur—from broken bones, torn ligaments, and pulled muscles to hypothermia and heat exhaustion (which marathoner Gabriela Andersen-Schiess succumbed to at the 1984 Summer Olympics). Knowing what these ailments look like and what they feel like, as well as understanding what causes them (and the signals that warn of their approach), will aid you in the safe pursuit of endurance.

We'll answer common questions people have about exercise, including how endurance athletes eat and go to the bathroom during an event, why people wear sweat clothes, when to work out, and how endurance improves the sex lives of these athletes.

By sharing the magic of endurance and bringing you as close as humanly possible to an understanding of that magnificent, unimaginable effort that is characterized by endurance, we hope that you will be inspired to find endurance in yourself—to tap your potential, test your limits, and watch the results spill over into every area of your life.

PART I
The Mind

1

"I Did It!"

"I knew it could be done, it had to be done and
I did it."

—*Gertrude Ederle, after becoming the first woman to
swim the English Channel in 1926*

You can do anything you set your mind to. The feelings that accompany any accomplishment in which you push yourself are wonderful, powerful, and inspiring. *These initial feelings of satisfaction give you a taste for what it's like to push yourself and motivate you to do more.* Taking life to the limit has a positive cyclical effect: The more you do, the more you discover you *can* do and the more you *want* to do.

Testing Your Limits
for the First Time

No one wakes up one day and runs fifty miles, swims the Channel, or finds him- or herself president of a company. In every career there is a series of small triumphs, each involving greater distances, longer hours, tougher obstacles. None, however, replaces the thrill of the first time, when the barriers fall away and the body, or the mind, realizes that *there are no limits*.

Discovering Your Staying Power

One year before I swam the English Channel, I had never swum over one hour in my life. In my case an accident prompted me to discover my staying power. I was performing on Broadway at the time and swimming about one mile a day for fitness and pleasure. I was thinking about increasing my workout and needed an excuse to do it. Then a swimming companion, who averaged two miles a day, broke his wrist. I was sorry that he had hurt himself and felt terrible that he would be unable to swim for six weeks. As a tribute I began swimming his distance.

Two miles of swimming was double my usual workout and quite a jump. But it was easy. I had never tried swimming so far and was surprised that in less than three weeks two miles became part of my regular routine. The surprise turned into a glint in my eye as I began to wonder, "How far could I go if I had no time limits?"

I chose a day and put myself to the test. I decided that I would swim five miles. One mile of swimming is equivalent to four miles of running, so my five miles was equal to a twenty-mile run, practically a marathon. I jumped into the water and swam for over two and a half hours: five slow, easy miles. When I was through, I wanted to jump in the air, raise my fist, and shout for everyone to hear: "I did it!" I would utter the same words one year later when I touched shore at Cape Gris-Nez after my eighteen-hour swim across the English Channel.

"I Did It!"

That first "I did it" is exciting and frightening and wonderful because you're not sure you have it in you. You don't know until you have actually run or swum or cycled or finished law school or had a baby that you can do it. You might believe you have the ability in your gut somewhere, but until you test it and actually get to the other side or finish a race and say "I did it," you just don't know for sure. *Completion of the task is the only way to earn true knowledge of your ability.*

Pushing Yourself
at Your Own Speed

Sometimes all we need is an excuse to test our limits for the first time. It doesn't matter how far you're going. And it doesn't matter what anyone else is doing. Pushing yourself is pushing yourself. The feeling is exalting to people at any fitness level. Judith Zimmer, my coauthor, tested her limits during her first five-mile run, and I was flattered to share it with her.

As Judith tells it:

I was a beginning runner, averaging about two or three miles a few times a week, and I was training for my first five-mile race.

Julie told me that I could double my distance without hurting myself. The race was three weeks away. Julie invited me to go to Central Park with her for a practice five-mile run.

Now? Why now? If it had been up to me, I would have procrastinated, been nervous about not being ready. But with Julie standing there, waiting for an answer, it felt like now or never. The time was right.

An hour later, she was waiting for me at the entrance to the park. The lap around Central Park's reservoir is about 1.6 miles; Julie planned to do a four-loop workout, 6.4 miles. My test would be three loops, 4.8 miles. We began running, Julie chatting gaily as we went. I loped along beside her, doing my best to match her pace and keep up my end of the conversation. Lap two was longer. I was quiet, concentrating on the pain. My calves were aching; my feet were hot and sweaty from hitting the dirt. I could easily stop, I told myself. It was that simple. I can walk. I can forget about this mess—my legs with their dull throb, Julie talking. It hurt too much. What was the point? Why was I out there? But I was more than halfway there, so I figured I may as well finish.

On our third lap Julie needed to pick up her pace and went ahead. When she left, I faced the narrow bridle path alone. I noticed the light above the trees and saw the shadows on the buildings outside the park. A runner I knew whooshed past me. I continued. I forgot about the pounding in my legs. I thought about Julie stroking up every inch of the East River in her swim twice around Manhattan and how much that probably hurt. Although my laborious five miles were peanuts compared to Julie's twelve- and twenty-one-hour swims, it seemed as though the inches flying past my feet were the same ones that she'd passed in the Channel and Manhattan swims. Certainly the emotions were the same.

I rounded the bend and realized that I was almost there. Our starting point was only sixty yards away. I suddenly felt light and free, felt as though I could fly. Out of the dusk Julie was running toward me. I grinned at her, spread my arms wide, and yelled, "I did it." She gave me the thumbs-up signal and continued on. Later, she told me that she had changed direction to catch my triumph.

It happened again to me in a freshwater lake. I set out to swim to the other side, a half mile, without thinking that it was too far or that I couldn't make it.

"I Did It!"

Stroking back across, I realized that if I set my mind to it, I, too, could swim the English Channel. It was that close.

There's always excitement and satisfaction in watching yourself go a little farther. It's similar to the thrill of any first-time accomplishment: cooking a three-course gourmet dinner, closing a deal, publishing an article. Hannah Rivers, a young free-lance writer from New York City, explains:

I had always wanted to be a writer. When I was young, I dreamed and fantasized about being a writer. Every year on my birthday, it was my wish when I blew out the candles.

As to the practical side of writing, I worked at it for years. I was editor of my high school newspaper and an English major in college. I took a job on a community newspaper and then worked for a national magazine. Here was my chance, I thought, as I opened the mail, typed manuscripts, and read other writers' masterpieces.

I kept my eyes open, using every chance I had to figure out what ingredients went into selling a magazine article. I planned and plotted my own article. Finally, I came up with an idea—something that was so way out that it hadn't been done before, or at least not in a long time. I asked my boss if I could write the article myself instead of giving it to another writer. She said I'd have to convince her—in a page—that the article would be worthwhile and that I could write it.

For a week, I slaved over those words; I had never chosen 250 words so carefully. When my boss returned the proposal to me with "Go ahead" printed across the top, I thought I would burst. I had sold an idea to a national magazine! I had gone from just wanting to be a writer to being a writer with an assignment.

A few months later, seeing my byline in the magazine was the icing on the cake. My dream had come true—I had done it!

You can experience personal triumph in any field. Most people—if they think hard enough—will remember when it happened to them.

Chris Files, from Cleveland, Ohio, had never sold anything in her life and had no sales experience when she became account manager for a small clothing import business which was just getting off the ground. As one of only two salespeople and claiming New York City, the fashion capital of the country, as her territory, Chris felt as though the success or failure of the company was literally sitting on her shoulders.

I felt as though it would be me who would make or break the company—which is a lot of pressure. The thing that was most difficult [about getting started during the first week of work] was that it was a competitive industry. No one will whisper a word about what's going on. You can't go to the library and get a book about the best stores in town. I knew Bloomingdale's and Saks, but I knew nothing about the good specialty shops.

I learned the hard way—by walking the streets, going into shops cold, and saying "Hi"; presenting me, my company, my line, and trying to make sales.

The second week [on the job] I was determined. I walked into thirty stores and ended up doing $10,000 in sales. I was excited. I felt as though I was personally responsible for bringing a product to New York City. Our company was in business in New York!

Inspired by Your Own Success
to Do More

Once you push back your limits for the first time, you've opened up the door of possibilities. You want to know how much farther you can go. "I think the big 'wow' never stops. It shouldn't," says triathlete Lyn Brooks. *"There are a lot of things out there to do."* One of the "things out there" that Lyn discovered was the Ultimate triathlon, a three-day stage race which included swimming 4 miles, biking 155, and running 31. Of the Ultimate, Lyn says, "I had never done any of those distances before. It was a thrill, a new venture. It was, again, what are your limits?"

You'll find that challenging yourself is not a one-time episode. It's continual. *You become addicted to the rewarding feelings you get* and the rigorous schedule that gets you to your goal. The process becomes as pleasurable as attainment of the goal. One challenge leads to another. You want to do more.

When P. J. Johnson joined a major international sports agency, his main task was to discover and promote sporting events that were not well known. Within a very brief time he brought bicycle racing and a midwestern sport called tractor pulling into the firm. "To be able to come into the leading firm [of its kind] in the world and to be able to research and then put together commercial sponsorship and make the sport commercially viable—that was an acorn. I don't think there are too many around. *That's what keeps you going. It makes you go out and find more,"* concludes P. J.

The confidence you discover from pushing yourself spills over into every other area of life.

Mike Frankfurt is a partner in a Manhattan law firm which specializes in the entertainment and communications field. At age forty-nine he runs races of various distances—

from short fun runs to marathons to fifty-mile races. Running makes him feel good about himself, and that helps him in his work. "What I do basically," explains Mike, "is deal with other people's problems. The essence of doing that is to have the people you're trying to help feel confident that you're telling them to do the right thing. That's a security you're trying to give out. And you can only do that if you believe it. I think there's a confidence that comes from being able to do things. Your first marathon or ultra-marathon does strike you as, 'I did that. I can do anything.' That 'anything' starts encompassing intellectual things, not just physical things."

Proving Yourself to Yourself

Another reason for taking on new challenges and testing yourself over and over again is that you may not be sure you *can* do it again. You may have done it once, but you reason that it was on that day, with that weather, with those tides, that crew. Many 1984 Olympic gold medalists must admit to themselves—"Yes, I have this gold medal, but if the Russians had been there, or the East Germans, would the gold have been mine?"

What if? What would have happened under a different set of circumstances? The need to conquer doubts keeps you testing your abilities again and again. You're never finished. If you were, you'd stop growing and trying altogether. As they say in the theater, "You are only as good as your last review."

At the age of sixteen Cindy Nicholas, of Toronto, Canada, completed her first long-distance open-water swim across Lake Ontario. Four years later, in 1978, Cindy was named Queen of the English Channel after completing her sixth successful crossing. She holds the record for the most Channel crossings for a woman (nineteen) and the most two-way crossings for a man or woman (five).

Cindy was a trained sprint swimmer who knew she had a knack for long-distance swimming. But after her first swim—across Lake Ontario—she wasn't sure she could do it again.

"When I did the English Channel for the first time," says Cindy, "I got in the water and wondered whether my first swim was a fluke, first-time enthusiasm, or real talent. I wasn't sure I could keep doing fifteen-hour swims or swims that were not calm or warm. If you threw in a variable like jellyfish, seaweed, or colder water, I wasn't sure I could actually do it. It wasn't until after the first Channel swim that I could look back to Ontario and say, I guess it wasn't a fluke. From then on I knew I could do a twenty-one-mile swim."

That Triumph Belongs
to You Alone

Each victory is yours, each and every special one of them. Says triathlete Lyn Brooks about her first marathon: "I finished, turned around, and was overwhelmed. I kept saying to myself, 'You ran twenty-six miles *all by yourself.*' That's the feeling that's so nice. *You* do it. People help you and it's a cooperative effort, but it's your body out there."

That undeniable feeling gives you satisfaction, self-confidence, and renewed self-esteem. Chris Files' experience entering New York City's marketplace fostered positive feelings about herself: "Selling taught me how to accomplish something on my own initiative. It's given me a sense of power. I know now that I can go out there and accomplish something concrete—on my own."

The feelings are so special that you are certain that no one else has ever had them quite that way before. Like first love, you will relish, savor, and carry those feelings with you always.

When you're in the middle of some unresolvable problem or life looks dismal, you can look back and bring forth those three little words. "Remember that day. On *that* day 'I did it.' " *You'll find that you feel strong, capable, and better able to meet the next challenge.*

2

Training: The Mental Process

In our society everyone wants to be successful. In sports that means getting out there and going all out to win.

But there are different kinds of success: One is competing against other people and being the best of the pack. *The other is challenging yourself and being the best you can be.*

The emergence of marathons, triathlons, and other endurance events all over the world suggests that people are discovering the kind of success that comes from challenging themselves—even though it has nothing to do with winning. They're finding that pushing themselves to get to the finish line is just as valid an effort as getting there first.

Besides, how can you tell the 14,590 1984 New York City Marathon participants who finished (16,315 runners competed in all) but didn't place first, second, or third that they weren't *successful* in the marathon? And what can you do but *applaud* the 600,000 participants who crossed a finish line in 1984 after completing triathlons of various distances? The boom in endurance sports indicates that athletes of all ages are interested in pushing their bodies to the limit for the sheer pleasure of *finishing* an event, not winning it.

Finishing Versus Winning

During the 1984 Summer Olympics I was asked several times why I wasn't competing. Wasn't I a swimmer and a good one? The questions frustrated and confused me. Often, people don't understand the concept of a solo endurance endeavor. Before my double swim around Manhattan, people urged me on by saying, "Go out and win!"

Win *what*? I wasn't racing anyone. There was no clock to beat. That is the major difference between the Olympic-caliber athletes and me. We all put in long hours, sweat a lot, and love what we do. But they train to go fast and win. I don't. They were born with speed. I wasn't. Their goals, based on their natural talents, are different from mine. Our training gets both of us where we're going—they just get there a lot faster.

I am more like the middle-of-the-packer than the elite athlete. I'm interested in setting personal goals for myself and working hard to attain them. My goal is to get to the other side without hurting myself. I train to *finish*.

But can you be satisfied with just finishing? Can you psych yourself up for it and not let the need to win impede your progress? Men or women who have been raised to view competition and winning as inherent to sports might have difficulty adjusting their mind-sets to the glories of *finishing*. But if they try to separate themselves from their

24

opponents and concentrate on enjoying what they're doing, they should be able to discover a new pleasure for themselves. That pleasure has nothing to do with winning and everything to do with *participating*.

Sit near the finish line of any marathon and you'll see the pleasure of participating. Watch the runners as they end their race. Most are smiling. Ask them—or anyone handing in a project on deadline, finishing a drawing, or seeing a cured patient walk out of the hospital—ask them how they feel. They probably feel pretty good about themselves. They've gone from a starting point to an end point. They've determined those starting and ending points and gotten there on their own.

When you set individual goals and reach them, you are a winner within the context of what you set out to do. Finishing is a personal triumph. "If you race to win and you don't win, where does that leave you? That's kind of a dead end," explains long-distance cyclist and triathlete John Howard. "I look for personal victory. A sense of accomplishment comes from knowing it was your best effort."

Just putting yourself on the line, commanding your mind or your body to perform, and giving your best effort is a celebration of yourself, of your capabilities, of being alive. "I think every finish line is an accomplishment. Just getting to it," says triathlete Lyn Brooks. "To me, the icing on the cake is to win. But I never come across a finish line feeling like a loser. Ever."

The Process of Getting There

The path most marathoners take to get to the finish line is similar to the path it takes to accomplish anything. It involves two factors:

- *Direction:* knowing what your goal is and what you want to do
- *Drive:* using your energy and your willpower to get to that goal

Direction is knowing *where* you're going. Drive is commitment, discipline, willpower, stick-to-itiveness. Drive and direction go together. You can have lots of drive, but without direction your energy will have you running in circles. Similarly, the worthiest goal in the world isn't worth a damn without the drive to proceed toward it.

Using Drive and Direction

All my life I have been goal-oriented. I would see something I wanted and figure out the fastest, least painful way to get it. When I first came to New York City, I had direction: I wanted to earn my living in the theater. I also had drive: the determination to stick to my goal.

I learned by trial and error and by persisting how to use my drive to chart the course to my goal. I discovered that there was a strategy behind the process of auditioning for a part, landing the role, rehearsing it into a disaster-free opening night, and keeping the job for as long as the show ran.

What worked for me was going to every audition that seemed appropriate for my talents, consistently sending out pictures and résumés, and maintaining regular contact with my agents. In about six months the agents and directors I had auditioned for knew who I was and what I could do. I began working. From then on, one job led to the next. My first job was a chorus role in a large out-of-town musical; next, a major role in a small musical, and so on right up to

26

Broadway. As I went to more and more auditions, performed regularly, and worked with different talented directors, my technique improved and my skill developed.

Stage one of the performing process was auditioning; stage two was rehearsal. While rehearsing my first show, I wanted desperately to please the director, keep the job, and perform well. Little details—showing up on time, preparing my lines and lyrics, working privately on the dance steps I always tripped over—set me apart as being reliable and hardworking. I left personal problems at home and concentrated as singularly on my work as I could.

Sighting a goal, figuring out the course, and following it with discipline and commitment were my greatest talents. No one told me what to want or how much to love what I did. On occasion, I received advice, but what I learned most of all was that you can achieve just about anything if you want it badly enough and work consistently toward it. The same principles applied when I set off to swim the English Channel.

The 13 Components
of Endurance

In sports the *training* process is clear and precise. Your goal is the event itself; the process of getting there is the training. There was no secret to my successful completion of the English Channel swim. The only trick was in plotting a proper course and following it. I adhered to a rigorous training program—a process which can be applied to any goal. Using my program for the Channel swim as a model, you'll see how the process of getting anywhere simply requires a good formula. Following it will provide the desired result: a successful completion.

1. SETTING A GOAL

We spend our lives working toward a series of goals. Some are big and take years—like becoming a lawyer. Others are smaller and take less time—like a lawyer working on a particular case.

Setting a goal is something you have to do for yourself. Other people can advise you, but it must be your decision to move into action. Only you know what you want and what you feel passionate about pursuing.

What the goal is, is not always as important as just having a goal and going after it. Some people get so caught up in selecting the right goal that they can't decide on any and end up stalling or doing nothing. Sometimes just pushing ahead or challenging yourself can inspire you to find a goal that you really want to pursue—or at least help you sift out what you *don't* want.

In sports—as in anything else—*it is important to set realistic goals and accept any physical, emotional, and intellectual limitations that you have.* I knew I wasn't a fast swimmer, but I discovered that I could last a long time. I am an extremist by nature. When I was a kid and fell in love with theater, I dreamed of performing on Broadway. It seemed only natural that when I fell in love with marathon swimming, I would dream of the English Channel.

Well, I made it to Broadway. It was while I was there that I became interested in long-distance swimming and made a New Year's resolution to leave the show and commit the next seven months to full-time training for my endurance project—swimming the English Channel. The goal was set. All that remained was to map a course and follow it.

2. RESEARCH: KNOW ALL YOU CAN ABOUT YOUR SUBJECT

I knew next to nothing about long-distance swimming

when I decided to swim the English Channel. I began my research by writing to everyone I could think of who might know something about the subject. I scoured New York's libraries. I read magazine articles about swimming, including one about Cindy Nicholas' training. I also read about professional long-distance swimmers' training programs in *Wind, Waves and Sunburn,* a treatise on long-distance swimming. I traveled to Fort Lauderdale, Florida, to visit the International Swimming Hall of Fame and to talk to its executive director, Buck Dawson.

You can never know too much about your subject. Usually, when you are excited about a project, you are eager to find out as much as you can. You'll find that *other people who are in the same field as you or interested in the same subject are often your greatest source of information.* "Lawyers call other lawyers," explains Mike Frankfurt. "You rely on what you know and what other people know. It's the same thing in running. Old-timers will tell you one thing about this or that that will help you."

Soon, just by talking to people and gathering and digesting so much information, you'll become a bit of an expert yourself.

3. ASSESSING YOUR STARTING POSITION

When I first started planning for my own swim, I had to be realistic about myself: What was my ability as a swimmer? I had to face facts: I had a weak stroke and zero experience in cold, open, ocean water. I had learned to swim as a child and simply swam for pleasure. I had no formal training at all. I'd never swum with a team or been coached.

When you're preparing yourself for a challenge, it's not the time for fantasies or boasting or bragging. You might impress other people, but *you must evaluate how equipped*

you truly are and how ready you are to face the challenge.
You'll waste little time and set up the right strategies if you
can assess your abilities honestly.

4. Developing Strategy

I took all the information I had gathered about long-
distance swimming and what I knew about myself as a
swimmer and devised a training program that would get me
from England to France.

I read over the various training regimens of the swimmers, taking into account what event they were training for
and what their particular backgrounds were, then compared
these to my own swimming history. Cindy Nicholas was a
trained sprint swimmer and did about three workouts a day,
four miles per workout. Her barest minimum was seven
miles a day. I couldn't compare myself to her.

Then I received a very informative letter from Doc
Councilman, who in 1979, at the age of fifty-eight, became
the oldest man to swim the Channel. He trained for fourteen
months, starting with 2 miles per day and clocking in a total
of 50 miles for the first month. He gradually upped his
mileage by 10 miles each month, until the last month he
logged in 190.

His training regimen made sense to me. Unlike the other
swimmers who were putting in high daily mileage at the
outset, his regime started small and grew, adding more and
more miles. It seemed like the best way for me to train.
Since I had only seven months in which to prepare and I was
about half his age, I cut Doc's program in half.

Strategy is an important part of the process. It gives you
something to stick to, an outline to follow. *Commit yourself
to your strategy and have faith in it when you feel your focus
slipping. Stick with it and your goal will be within range.*

5. Putting Your Plan into Action: Start Slowly and Build

When I began training, I was swimming two miles a day for fitness. In keeping with Doc Councilman's regimen, I would stick with my two miles a day and log in about fifty miles in the first month. I would be building on my base and would slowly increase my distance until I was swimming four to six miles a day.

I needed to establish a sound mileage base. It had to be done gradually and steadily, like putting money in the bank. The greater your capital, the greater your interest. Too much too fast would break me down, wear me out, and/or kill my keen desire. Building a fortune takes time and patience.

Start small and build. Each small step is an accomplishment and a building block for the next step. If you look at the whole process, you might feel overwhelmed. It's like standing at the foot of a mountain: If you look straight up at the top, you are bound to get dizzy. Take it step by step, boulder by boulder, day by day, and you'll get to the top sooner or later.

6. Be Prepared: Look at the Whole Package and Anticipate Obstacles

I took my training seriously. I meant business. I knew the obvious obstacles—20.5 miles of ocean, 55° to 65° water temperatures, currents, tides, heavy boat and freighter traffic—and *I had to be ready for them.*

I knew that accumulating mileage was only the beginning. Training must include as many as possible of the conditions that will be encountered in the actual event. The fewer surprises, the better. To ignore any of the elements can be both foolish and dangerous. I had to be prepared for cold, open, rough water, for swimming over eight hours at a time, and for swimming at night.

I began with a test of my mental ability during a long-distance swim by completing a twelve-hour pool swim. I found that the longer I swam, the more I loved it. I did one long swim of eight to ten miles once a week or once every two weeks as a regular part of training. The purpose of these long swims was to discipline my mind to put up with four to five hours of straight, repetitious activity.

I learned to swim in the ocean off the coast of Fort Lauderdale, Florida, and Newport, Rhode Island. (The locations were chosen because I could stay with friends there.) Buck Dawson invited me to train at Ak-o-Mak, his Canadian swimming camp. There I swam in a 58° to 62° lake and put in what I call special training efforts. These were days set aside from routine training, specifically geared toward mastering factors unique to the challenge ahead. For me, these special training sessions included a nine-hour open-water swim and a five-hour night swim. (Many swimmers are afraid of the dark, fearful of things unseen lurking beneath the water's surface.) Swimming at two miles an hour as I do, I am not fast and knew that my Channel swim might involve dark hours. I wanted to be prepared. I trained with an escort boat, through waves, wind, and heavy rains to ready myself for whatever the Channel might offer.

Another part of my preparation was to gain weight before the swim. I added fifteen pounds to my 5'3" frame for greater insulation against the cold. I also knew that long-distance swimmers can burn as many as 750 calories per hour. Therefore, you need extra weight to start with so you've got something to lose.

I knew that I would have to replenish my energy during the swim. But I didn't know what kinds of foods I would want to eat in the middle of the Channel. I used my twelve-hour pool swim to experiment with feedings. I discovered that hot chocolate, tea with milk and honey, and Gatorade gave me the energy I needed. The liquids stayed down and I liked them. I have since expanded my feedings to include bananas, baby food, juice, and water.

Be fully prepared for whatever you're getting yourself involved in and anticipate obstacles before they happen so they don't take you by surprise. If you've trained in all kinds of weather, you will know how your body responds to different climates and adjust your pace accordingly.

It helps if you can be flexible and open-minded about your strategy. If you're welded to its structure, you might miss the opportunity to prepare for obstacles. Your strategy is your own. It should be tailored to your progress.

When you want something very badly, obstacles don't stop you from getting to your goal. On the contrary, they inspire and challenge you. Hurdling them becomes an integral part of the process.

7. Draw on Past Experience: Incorporate What You Already Know

As I trained, I drew on my past experience in every field. For example, when I was in college, I worked every Friday night at a twenty-four-hour bakery on the graveyard shift, 11 P.M. to 7 A.M. Going without sleep one night a week was part of my regular routine. I didn't know then that this training in sleep deprivation would come in handy when I had to swim for twenty-one hours.

You know more than you think you do. Achieving something once gives you knowledge about yourself and your abilities. Knowing you accomplished something in the past also gives you the courage and inspiration to do it again (see chapter 1). Remind yourself of past achievements or tough situations you had to endure.

When I have trouble on a four- or five-hour swim, I

remind myself of the Channel or my first twelve-hour pool swim and the trouble disappears. What aspects of your nature did you learn about when you tested your limits? What personal strengths or attributes made you successful?

- Positive outlook
- Strength of will and determination
- High self-esteem
- Assertiveness
- Decisiveness

Try to apply what you learned to the challenge you now face. If you pushed back your limits once, chances are you can do it again.

8. GETTING ENOUGH REST AND PROPER NUTRITION

Whether it's off-season or full-time training, I always pay attention to rest and the way I eat. I stick to healthy whole foods with an emphasis on carbohydrates, whole-grain rice, fish, poultry, and tons of fruits and vegetables. I don't eat most refined sugars and flours, caffeine, chemicals, or alcohol. I drink lots of juice and water to keep my system clean and to restore the fluids lost during workouts.

I make sure I get enough sleep every night and take one or two days off every week. Rest and recovery are as much a part of building capital as actual training. Going full force all the time is a sure road to injury and mental burnout.

Rest and recovery should be part of everyone's life—no matter what goal you are striving for. Sleeping enough to feel alert and rested, eating nutritiously, and relaxing one's mind restore energy.

9. PRACTICING MENTAL PREPARATION

The winter before I swam the English Channel, I took an eight-hour walk around Manhattan. I wanted to do some-

thing other than swimming, but just as long and arduous. I
imagined that it was good preparation for my swim. It was a
cold, snowy day. I knew, obviously, that walking around in
the snow wasn't going to increase the strength in my arms
or improve my swimming. It did, however, condition me
mentally for the difficulty of the task that lay ahead. About
four hours into the walk, my feet were getting numb, I was
in a lousy neighborhood, and I began to wonder what the
point of all this was. I considered hopping a bus. But I'd
only been walking for four hours and didn't think I'd been
out long enough to do me any good, so I stuck with it.

*Mental endurance is behind every great effort, whether
it's physical or intellectual.* Sticking with your project—not
giving up—takes practice (see chapter 5). The better you
understand what it feels like to endure—or to continue on
when you want to give up—the easier it will be for you to
do it.

10. FINAL PREPARATION: DO A DRESS REHEARSAL

In the middle of the sixth month of my training I went to
England. I spent my remaining training weeks in the Channel. It is a good idea, whenever possible, to test the waters
before event day. Knowledge of what you are getting into is
invaluable. The actor usually gets a dress rehearsal or two
before he goes on for opening night. Performers have been
known to go without dress rehearsal and manage to get
through without falling off the stage or forgetting lines. But
if you've got the chance, *give yourself all the extra preparation you can afford—if only for peace of mind.*

11. TAPERING YOUR TRAINING TO CONSERVE ENERGY

The end of each training season, just prior to the event,
is an important period of time called the taper. About a

week before the event, athletes decrease activity and take it easy to allow their bodies to conserve energy. (Some inexperienced athletes cram a lot of miles into their last week, trying desperately to make up for training deficiencies. But if you are not in good enough shape one week before the event, you are certainly not going to get there in the remaining time.) The taper is used to store rest and glycogen; athletes call it "maximizing the energy reserve." Train just enough to stay loose, confident, and strong; "just enough" will vary according to the individual. Be sure you have adequate food and rest.

Similarly, you can taper for a particularly rigorous workweek. Give yourself extra time to relax, get ample sleep, and eat well before pushing to your limit. Like the athlete, you can help your mind and body on the job by maximizing your energy reserve.

12. Seeing the Goal to Completion

By the seventh month, I had trained in just about every possible condition the Channel could throw at me. I had a solid distance base of over eight hundred miles. My money was in the bank. It was time to draw on the interest.

If you've followed your strategy, you should be ready and well prepared to undertake your project. Sometimes you are so ready for your "event" that pulling it off is actually easier than the process you went through to get there.

13. Planning the Next Challenge: Reassess Progress/Success

After the swim to France, I reviewed my program. I had come a long way from the young woman who swam two miles a day for fitness. I had mastered ocean swimming and had a solid distance base under my belt. I felt as though I had a formula that worked for me.

The next season, when I decided to swim twice around Manhattan, I had to consider what the Channel swim had taught me and how I would modify my training to accommodate the special needs of the Manhattan Double. A swim around Manhattan required beating the tide change at the Battery. If I was too slow, I wouldn't make it. My training would have to emphasize more speed work. I began doing interval training, which involved swimming series of fast laps (called a set) with short rest intervals in between them.

Planning your next challenge is similar to the earlier step of assessing your position. This time, however, you're ahead of the game. You have knowledge from the first challenge. Like the athlete who has built up a strong, lean, flexible body, you also have built up a wealth of experience. You know what strategy is and how to stick to it. You've seen how the formula works: how drive and direction combine to get you where you want to go. You have a base to build on.

3

The Techniques That Develop Mental Toughness

Deep desire as a primary motive can get you pretty far, but, as they say, love isn't everything. How do you get through the long hours of training for a marathon, preparing a case, or pulling an all-nighter? What do you *think* about during all those hours? How do you resist the temptation to quit?

The Event May Not Be as Difficult as the Training

For the athlete, occupying the mind during a sporting event or race is not *always* difficult: The excitement of the moment, the competition, and concentrating on form all help fill the time. What is difficult—and what, in fact, takes more preparation and discipline—is getting through the training hours: for the ultra-athlete, those four to eight hours a day, five to six days a week.

It is these hours that stereotype the endurance athlete as self-involved and lonely. And it is precisely these hours that the athlete alternately longs for and dreads. They confound, fortify, and excite. You have to like yourself to spend that much time alone. You need imagination not to get bored.

The same is true for any kind of mental marathon. The trial itself is easier to get through than the hours it took to prepare for it. Rehearsals take longer than the show. How do you keep yourself going? How do you keep your mind on the task at hand?

Training the Mind
to Get You Through

Like the body, the mind must be trained to cooperate in the effort. Properly trained, your mind will help keep you going by

- Renewing optimism in yourself
- Reducing distraction and interference
- Reestablishing your desire and determination

Here are some steps you can take to toughen your mind to the task at hand:

STEP 1. REMEMBER YOUR GOAL

When finishing seems particularly hard and all the pep talks in the world can't seem to persuade you to go on, remember your goal. Your goal is a commitment—to yourself, to your boss, to the people counting on you. Keeping your goal in mind gives you something to focus on and something to feel committed to. *Your goal and your desire to see the thing through become your reasons to keep going.*

STEP 2. BE AWARE OF WHERE YOUR MIND IS

When you are in the middle of a project and you feel your attention wandering, stop and ask yourself why you're losing concentration. Why have you slowed down while running? Are you thinking about running or are you looking at someone? Are the noises outside bothering you while you're trying to work on a Sunday afternoon? *Just becoming aware that your mind is wandering can help you to pull your attention back when you feel it slipping away.*

STEP 3. DEVELOP YOUR CONCENTRATION

For the athlete, actor, or cashier, concentration can mean preventing a bicycle accident, keeping a job, or saving money by punching the right register keys. Concentration means focusing your attention and energy on something specific. It is a skill you can improve if you are aware of your attentional strengths and weaknesses. It is an invaluable tool when giving your all to a job or project. Here are two examples of how people use concentration:

Paul Asmuth describes how he concentrated during a swimming race around Atlantic City: "When the sun was out, I just wanted to stay behind the boat. My boat was the blue one, except where some paint had peeled off on the keel that made it white. All I concentrated on was following that little white spot on the keel. It held my mind for hours. When I started concentrating on that, I really started moving well in the ocean and getting into my stroke. Nothing else filled my mind. That took a lot of concentration because the water was murky. Every time I finished my stroke I had to look for it."

As a commodities trader, Vicky Aden's use of focus is a natural part of her job. "Trading is mentally and physically very demanding," she explains. "You are usually doing at least three things at once, and you have to be able to expand that to fifteen at a time. You can easily be on two phones at once while three or four more are ringing while you're watching the market and while you're writing or time-stamping something. And things are going on around you. You have to be able to focus and prioritize instantly. That takes discipline.

"There's going to be a moment when you have to be absolutely conscious of what you're hearing in your right ear—say it's a client—and be able to turn him off for a split second and listen to what is going on in your left ear, which is probably the market. And then turn them both off and be able to look at what's on the screen in front of you. Then you shut that whole thing down and listen to what someone is yelling to you from the other side of the room. It's almost like a symphony and you're the conductor."

Understanding What Kind of Concentration Is Needed for Your Activity

In the examples above, Paul Asmuth and Vicky Aden were both using concentration skills, although each one was employing a different focus.

Sports psychologist Andrew Jacobs, founder of the Winning Edge of Kansas City, Missouri, works as a consultant to athletes and businesses interested in enhancing their athletic or corporate performance. One of the areas Dr. Jacobs emphasizes to his clients is concentration. He categorizes four types of attentional focuses in order to help clients recognize their strengths and weaknesses. They are:

narrow, broad, internal, and external. With an understanding of what each focus is, you can recognize when your mind is using one or another and can gain some control over your mind's mechanisms.

- Narrow Focus   Used when you focus on only one specific idea, image, or object

- Broad Focus   Used when you focus on—and are able to take in—many things (ideas, objects) at one time

The Direction of Your Focus

- Internal Focus   Used when your attention is turned inward and you are more conscious of your own thoughts and feelings than of what is going on around you

- External Focus   Used when your attention is turned toward the events going on around you

Here are the ways these focus areas help you to carry out your activities:

Type of focus: Broad external
Used for: Being aware of everything going on around you
Used by: Runners and cyclists use this focus so they can pay attention to obstacles in their way. Also used by supervisors or people in managerial positions who must keep track of what other people

are doing. Anyone making a speech uses this focus to maintain awareness of how people are responding and to know what is going on around them.

Type of focus:	Broad internal
Used for:	Ability to analyze and to make decisions
Used by:	Anyone making decisions, planning or writing out a schedule. You use this focus to make connections and decisions and to bring pieces of information together.

Type of focus:	Narrow external
Used for:	Ability to focus on one thing that is outside you
Used by:	Anyone who is focusing on something in the distance, such as a golfer, tennis player, or baseball player who is preparing to hit or catch a ball. Also used during one-on-one conversations where you are looking at, and talking to, one person.

Type of focus:	Narrow internal
Used for:	Ability to think about only one thing at a time and to focus on that exclusively
Used by:	Anyone who is thinking about or developing one single topic or idea

How to Shift Your Focus

You can develop the focus that most suits your activity. Part of good concentration is being able to shift from one focus to another depending on what kind of focus is most appropriate to the situation.

"The key to good concentration skills is to know that you have to shift your attention span from one of these areas to another," explains Dr. Jacobs. "And realizing that there are specific times in every job or activity where one focus is more useful than another."

For example, during a one-on-one conversation, your focus shifts from your own thoughts to what the other person is telling you. If this shift does not take place, you can't fully assimilate the person's ideas, nor can you convey your own ideas intelligently. In an exercise class your focus moves from concentrating on your own movement to watching the instructor. If not, you can't be sure that you're doing the movement safely and with maximum health benefit.

When he runs, Stu Mittleman shifts his focus from narrow internal to a broad external. "I'm usually conscious of every time I take a step," says Stu. "I'm taking inventory, relaxing and stretching. I just try to be aware of everything that's happening. I'm constantly monitoring my body, checking other people, getting feedback on how I'm doing in terms of mileage and time, calculating when I need water, checking out breathing, breathing deeply. Am I relaxed? I'm checking my shoulders and my legs. I'm checking on the landing of my feet, making sure no blisters are developing."

How to Develop Your Focus

Make a list of the focuses your work or sport demands. Try to decide which attentional areas are your strengths and weaknesses. You'll find that just by being conscious of your mind's capabilities, your ability to use focus will improve.

STEP 4. MENTAL REHEARSAL

Call it mental rehearsal, visual imagery, or visualization. This is a technique used by athletes and businesspeople alike when they want to prepare themselves physically and mentally for an event that demands their whole attention and expertise.

I visualized my double swim around Manhattan at least fifty times before jumping into the East River. Coaches encourage athletes to picture the event in their minds before a race. The challenge then is to hold on to that image and concentrate on it.

Mental rehearsal works well in nonsports activities as well. "I use Sunday night to review the week and my schedule, rehearsing what I'll be thinking about over the week," explains P. J. Johnson, a sports marketing consultant and agent. "For example, I had to take a business call from London at 3 A.M. I woke myself up and was prepared. I knew what I was going to have to do. I had done the thinking ahead of time."

Here are four tips recommended by Dr. Jacobs, who works with athletes who use mental rehearsal before going to bed, before a nap, or before an event or game:

- Make sure you feel calm and relaxed. The ideal setting is a quiet room where you won't be disturbed. But you can practice visualization anywhere—on a bus, in a cab—as long as you are calm and relaxed.
- Begin by picturing yourself doing a movement or giving a presentation and doing it well. That successful image of yourself will give you a positive attitude about what you're going to do and will help you to bring to the actual event feelings of confidence, grace, and skill.
- Try visualizing yourself going through the race or the

presentation and making a mistake. How will you cope with that? Will you let your anger or frustration show? How will you cover up or excuse yourself? Being familiar with how you will react in an uncomfortable situation can help you to control your behavior and respond appropriately to whatever happens.

- Experiment to see how many times you need to repeat an image before it improves your ability. "It depends on the individual how many times you do it," says Dr. Jacobs. "When it helps them, people do it over and over again."

Tips for Staying Motivated

Life is too short to spend any of it being bored. To avoid boredom, it helps to love what you're doing and not waste time on things that don't move you toward your goal.

One or several of the following mind games may help:

1. If you're doing a constant, monotonous activity, use your time to let your mind create.

Endurance sports give you the time and luxury to engage in imaginary play. Most casual runners or mile-a-day swimmers agree that their greatest pleasure and main goal in working out is to relax their minds, solve problems, and unwind.

I use some of my swimming time to think, write, solve problems, and work out my anger and frustration. I have planned my entire life during a long swim, screamed at the man who stood me up for the second time, screamed at myself for letting him do it, and fantasized about what it would be like to be rich. I have sung songs, called to mind and replayed scenes from "Star Trek" episodes, and traveled to places that aren't found on my Neiman-Marcus globe.

"Dissociation" is the term sports psychologists use to describe the process of the mind detaching itself from what the body is doing. But be careful. Running, swimming, or performing any monotonous task can be dangerous if you aren't paying attention. Sports psychologists use the term "association" to describe a safer form of mental activity in which the mind continually shifts its focus; it wanders, but comes back to keep tabs on what the body is doing.

2. Learn to pace yourself by dividing a long-term goal into smaller ones.

Pacing yourself involves envisioning the entire project or long-term goal and dividing it into achievable portions. Each portion is a stepping stone leading you to the completion of your goal.

"In business I work with people on specific goals," explains Dr. Jacobs. "For example, suppose someone has five days to put together an ad campaign. That means that they're going to have to pace themselves each day. First they must sit down and decide on what the long-term goal is and what it's going to take to get the project done. Then they have to sit down and go through all that and plan it out."

The long-term goal that you're heading for is your prime motivator. It inspires you and keeps you going. But it isn't always easy to keep that goal in mind when it's so far away. "Running a marathon is a long-term goal," says Dr. Jacobs. "On a day-to-day basis you have to focus short-term. Take it two miles at a time. You use the short-term goals to reinforce yourself along the way. In business it's the same way: Everything you do that gets you closer to finishing is a short-term goal."

3. Keep track of your progress to keep motivation from sagging.

Record your progress in writing at the end of every week. It will give you a clear picture of what you're doing and the quality of your work. I keep records of hours and mileage spent on the course. It is exciting to watch them accumulate. When I've put in a few hundred miles, I think, "I could have swum from New York to Boston."

I have a log for my Nautilus routine that includes each machine, the weight I use, and how many repetitions I perform properly. Over the years I've watched my strength increase, plateau, peak, decline, and increase again. It keeps me on target and gives me tangible evidence that I'm working.

Keeping records of your daily activities and schedule will help you be prepared for the work that's coming up. You can pace yourself more evenly when it's mapped out clearly behind you—and ahead of you. "It's a good chastising item and a good discipline," says P. J. Johnson about his daily report of business activities." You're sometimes surprised when you thought you had done a lot. You say, 'Is this all I've done? I've spent too much time talking and listening.' You can be more focused; there's a lot of fluff in every day."

4. Break up the routine.

In some career situations it's not possible to break up your routine. You are expected to do the same job in the same way every day. But in cases where it is possible to change the pattern, try it. In sports, biking over the same terrain, running the same number of miles, or swimming the same stroke day after day is bound to get monotonous. Vary the distance you do in each workout. Do your weight stations in a different order. (This is only for advanced weight training; beginners should keep the order the same.) Fool the body now and then. Your mind will appreciate the change.

I needed to bike a lot of miles in preparation for the Ironman triathlon. Hundreds of loops in New York's Central Park drove me nuts. Sunday bike rides out of the city with a compatible biking partner were pleasurable, while fulfilling my mileage requirements.

Dancer and choreographer Rebecca Kelly handles both the business and the creative sides of her dance company. She finds both aspects different and challenging, and she's managed to use the difference to her advantage. "I get all hotted up about what I'm creating and then I have to do straightforward things like writing a letter. It relaxes my body. I'm relaxing one set of muscles and using another. They balance out. I'm constantly renewing myself. One of the reasons I have a lot of energy for everything I'm doing is that I can renew myself so easily."

5. Take advantage of the obstacles.

You do what you have to do to get where you want to go. Obstacles will present themselves along the way. Instead of letting them dishearten you or slow you down, use them to your advantage. They build strength and give you the edge over those who train only under sunny skies.

A cold, overcast, unpleasant day may seem like a great excuse to stay home. But it can also mean perfect conditions for special training. The more varied conditions you train under, the better prepared you are on event day. If you have weathered the rain, cold, excessive heat, and various other adverse situations in training, you will be better prepared to face them during the event.

49

During a race, Paul Asmuth takes comfort in the realization that everyone in the water is going through the same hardships. He draws strength from the fact that the fog is no less thick, the water no less cold, the waves no less rough for anyone else. He even goes a step further. When the fog rolls in, he uses what could be a distraction or handicap as a chance to put some distance between him and the guy trailing him. He knows everyone is having trouble seeing, so he concentrates all the harder, puts faith in his escort vessel and support crew, and plunges ahead. The rougher, colder, or tougher the conditions are, the better Paul will do.

In my biking I have actually begun to look forward to the uphills. The hard climb has the reward of the downhill, with the wind whizzing through my sweaty hair. Without uphills, there are no downhills.

6. Work with a trainer.

Support in any endeavor relieves stress, makes you feel less alone, and gives you some ideas you may not have come up with yourself. Working on a presentation with your boss or a coworker, or attending Weight Watchers groups, for example, gives your path different dimensions.

Some athletes won't train a single hour without a coach. Others know themselves quite well and prefer inventing their own workouts, with only occasional support or advice from a trainer.

In my case, I swim, bike, and run alone, but my Nautilus program is carefully supervised by my trainer. It is based on my needs and the goals of my season. He knows far more than I do about weight training and I follow his instructions with complete trust. Knowing that I will be taken through the weight routine, watched carefully to make sure I won't hurt myself, and encouraged all along the way helps me push toward my goal. I look forward to, and enjoy, the workouts.

Similarly, many people enjoy taking classes with a particularly inspiring teacher. They gain strength, energy, and motivation from everyone else sweating up a storm, or they work especially hard to please the teacher they like.

7. Get rest, take breaks.

Take a break now and then to help renew your energy. Dr. Jacobs advises his business clients to "take a relaxation break—give yourself time to take a breath and clear your mind. In essence, take your mind to the beach. Coming back, you'll be able to concentrate better."

Dr. Jacobs also suggests that people have a minimum of a half hour to an hour's worth of time to themselves every day. "People who take some time for themselves every day seem to be the ones who are happier and are able to maintain a better level of concentration."

4

Knowing How Far
Is Too Far:
Avoiding Burnout

Pushing yourself isn't easy. As appealing as the *idea* of striving toward a goal may seem, the actual process of getting there can be difficult, stressful, or painful. There is sometimes a big difference between how much you *want* to do and how much you *are able* to do. Knowing how much you can take on safely will help you push back your limits. *By pacing yourself, you'll avoid the dangers of burnout.*

Are You Pushing Too Much?

Too much of anything—even something like physical exercise, which is basically good for you—can be harmful.

In sports, overconfidence and zealousness can get you into trouble. You can easily overdo it by going out too fast in a race or putting in too many training hours. Continually throwing yourself into the sports arena without care as to how much you can handle can, in time, lead to injury. Often athletes are blinded to the signs of physical stress because of their enthusiasm and love of the sport—until they reach a point of burnout, where injury or illness forces them to bring their activity to a halt.

We see instances of burnout outside the sports arena as well. The executive who is driven to do more and more in less time is deemed a workaholic or called compulsive. Workaholics sometimes use work as an escape from other parts of their lives. They push without a particular plan of action. They could actually achieve more and remain mentally and physically healthy by altering their working hours, using time more efficiently, setting realistic goals, and keeping their priorities in perspective while they work.

DON'T CONFUSE TESTING YOUR LIMITS WITH OVERDOING IT

Pushing yourself to be the best you can be is not the same as compulsive, workaholic behavior—at least, it shouldn't be. That is a misconception of achieving. The best kind of effort is studied, controlled, and careful.

The ultra-athletes who have succeeded in safely pushing their bodies to the limit have given careful thought as to how to do it. Training is accomplished either systematically or not at all. Successful people in any field push forward *without injury to themselves and without neglecting other areas of their lives.*

The Positive Push: A Little Discomfort or Stress Can Work for You

Experienced athletes know that *some pain is an integral part of pushing back physical limits*. They draw a clear line, however, between dangerous pain and the pain or discomfort they must experience to grow and to go further. They know how to *use* discomfort to their advantage. What might look like masochism to the spectator is, to the athlete, a knowledge and trust in the reward beyond the pain. You cannot test your boundaries without feeling it.

"Normal endurance pain is temporarily uncomfortable or extreme anaerobic displeasure; it's something that has to be endured," explains John Howard. "The way you handle normal endurance pain is knowing when to back off. When things start hurting to the point where you feel a deep muscle fatigue, you pay attention to it. The body has enough mechanisms that tell you when it's shutting down. You tend to back off before you drop, so if you're watching out, you aren't at great risk of injuring yourself."

Most athletes learn through experience to listen to what their bodies are telling them and to be alert to the signals of trouble.

Symptoms of overdoing it in sports:

- Radical change in sleep habits (insomnia or sleeping more than usual)
- Irritability and restlessness
- Recurring minor injuries (see chapter 12)
- Uncontrollable weight loss
- Feeling of staleness

How Athletes Use Discomfort

Picture the athlete. She runs set after set of sixty-yard sprints. She rests between each one for ten or twenty seconds, then runs as hard as or harder than she ran before. Her pulse rises, sweat pours out, heart pounds, muscles burn as lactic acid builds up. She hurts. She hurts bad. She pushes still. Her body hurts so completely that she can't hurt any more unless she actually injures herself. This intense feeling will reach a sustained level, where it will not get any greater. When you hurt completely, in every fiber, you cannot hurt more.

Understanding this threshold is what gives the athlete the power to keep going. She knows not only that the pain will remain at a consistent level, a level she can endure, but that it is a *bridge*. She will push through this level into another place. She knows that a rush, a high, will replace the pain. She begins to look forward to the pain, knowing the tremendous joy of the place beyond it.

Stress: How to Use It to Your Advantage

Just as some pain is necessary for the athlete, a certain amount of stress is helpful in working situations. "A little bit of stress is good for you," explains Dr. Jacobs. "Our lives are full of stress. Stress is what motivates us to get going; stress is what keeps us going."

Positive stress can bring out the best in you. A little surge of adrenaline can give you a healthy mixture of tension and stimulation. (If you didn't experience any stress at all, you might feel bored or tired.)

A little stress can give you a surge of energy to catch a bus, to stand up in a meeting and give a stirring speech, to meet a deadline, to do your best when performing or in any situation where your work will be judged.

Too much stress, on the other hand, can be overwhelming. You need to find a healthy balance so that you can use stress before it uses you. "There's good stress and bad stress," says Dr. Jacobs. "It's good when it's helping us, it's bad when it's working against us. We have to learn to identify our peak levels of performance, where we are using stress to its peak level where it can be effective for us."

Like the athlete, you can listen to what your body is telling you about how stress affects you mentally and physically.

Stress causes chemical changes in the body which you notice immediately. This physiological reaction to stress or fear is called the fight or flight response. The following symptoms are the most common responses to stress:

- Increased heartbeat
- Elevated blood pressure
- Perspiration
- Inability to eat
- Restlessness
- Muscle tension

Unfortunately, the signs of stress are similar whether the stress is healthy or unhealthy, so you have to learn to identify the symptoms that indicate when you are using stress effectively and when you are faced with too much of it.

Here are some other negative physical and mental responses to stress which might affect you:

- Physical ailments
    Insomnia
    Headache
    Upset stomach
    Muscle stiffness
    Jaw, neck, or lower back pain

- Psychological ailments
  - Irritability
  - Anxiousness and inability to concentrate
  - Inability to relax
  - Excessive drinking, smoking
  - Loss of or increase in appetite

The Four Major Causes of Burnout and How to Pace Yourself to Avoid Them

When you expend energy, you want to make sure that you aren't going too far. Keep an eye on any tendencies you might have to make your drive turn against you. Spot the causes of burnout before burnout gets to you.

CAUSE 1. PUSHING YOURSELF BEYOND SAFE LIMITS

"Some people aren't satisfied with less than crashing," explains runner Stu Mittleman, who admits that he's "crashed and burned" in a few races, often those in which he found himself up with the leaders, got really excited, and kept going with them.

"I crashed when I did the 1980 fifty-mile race in the Athletic Conference Championship held in New York," says Stu. "I went out with the leaders and tried to hold a sub-six-minute pace. At the marathon point I fell apart, I crashed: I was almost unable to control bodily movements. Cramps started coming on. Picking up my leg became such a focused effort that I started to trip over my own feet and stagger." To avoid crashing dangerously, Stu realized what was happening and pulled back. He was able to complete the race, agonizingly but successfully.

CAUSE 2. FOCUSING ONLY ON THE GOAL AND IGNORING THE PROCESS

Often when you want something very badly, you don't have the patience to work for it. You may be in a hurry to succeed but are bored by the steps necessary to get to your goal. This can happen when you have only a superficial interest in your project and don't really enjoy the everyday process of what you are doing. "I've known people who want to be dancers but who don't want to do dancing. There's a big difference," says Rebecca Kelly.

Don't let impatience—wanting to get to your goal too quickly—ruin your effort. Overeagerness can kill many a good intention. Athletes learn that they have to back off— no matter how much they want to exercise—when their body says no to the effort. "There's a strong desire to keep performing at those top levels, but the body just isn't always there and ready," explains John Howard. "Part of being an endurance athlete is developing patience."

CAUSE 3. NOT LISTENING TO YOUR MIND'S OR BODY'S WARNINGS TO STOP OR SLOW DOWN

Even though your work habits might appear to other people as compulsive, only you can judge whether you have your work life under control. Rebecca Kelly doesn't doubt that some people think she is a workaholic, but she knows that her work is integrated into the rest of her life. "If my work damages my health or the health of the people around me, then I've overstepped some boundary," says Rebecca. "But as long as there is a balance of health and well-being, then what is compulsive? I don't set my sights on a goal that compels me to extreme behavior. I have a well-developed appetite for what I've chosen to do with my life and I do it with vigor."

CAUSE 4. DOING TOO MUCH OF THE SAME THING

Many runners and other sport-specific athletes who devote too much time to their sport can become unmotivated or fatigued by it. The solution? Turn to another sport. When they've exercised other parts of the body, they can return to the original sport with enthusiasm, ease, and a fit physique.

John Howard was, as he described in the July/August 1984 issue of *Ultrasport Magazine,* "buried" in bicycling. After twelve years as a specialized athlete, he found that "the narrowing experiential zone not only depressed me, it affected my competitive judgment." For the rest of his career, John alternated between cycling events and triathlons, which allowed him to cross-train in three sports and vary both the stress to his body and the stress to his mind.

Breaking up monotonous days and changing anything related to your work habits—your job, the people you socialize with, your office environment—can revitalize you. Integrating a fitness program into your daily regimen will help you to flex muscles while letting your mind take a rest.

Good Pacing Techniques

As they work out over a period of time, athletes find their winning pace. They find it by being sensible and using their heads. Knowing how far you can go and still feel comfortable is integral to pushing yourself.

Don't just dig in on the next task. Evaluate your work and work habits. How many hours of quality work can you put in? Where is the point of diminishing returns? Are you taking the necessary breaks to relax and refresh your mind?

Now that you are aware of the possible causes of burnout, try to adjust your attitude and behavior to pace yourself. Below are four questions to ask yourself to find out whether you are maintaining a good pace.

1. Are you pushing yourself gradually and allowing yourself to adapt to stress?

The process of pushing back limits involves a sequence of events: first feeling stressed mentally or physically and then slowly allowing the body to adapt to that level. When you can handle that same physical or mental load without feeling stressed, you know that your body has adapted and you can push it farther.

In sports this is known as the overload principle. It is most evident in progressive weight resistance, in which you stress your body with as much weight as it can handle. The next day, you allow your muscles to recover. Then you lift again. With this day-on, day-off exercise pattern, your body gradually adapts itself to the stress and soon you are able to lift more weight. The same principle operates in interval training, in which the body is stressed for short periods of time with rest intervals in between. The speed at which you can run or swim is gradually increased as the body adapts.

"If you take stress in little doses, your body's ability to adapt to being under stress changes. By stressing muscles, you grow," explains Dan Sikowitz, an exercise physiologist, who is the coordinator for the fitness evaluation program at the Biofitness Institute in New York City.

In a work situation think about stress the same way. Try to be aware of the amount you handle daily. If you know you have a particularly tough week ahead, apply the stress-adapt principle. During that week you will be increasing tension. Make sure you get adequate rest and relaxation afterward so that your stress level comes back down to normal and you recover. Gradually, you will feel more comfortable handling even higher levels. *Learning that you can control your reaction to stress* can help you adapt to difficult situations in a positive, healthy way.

2. *Is your drive to success healthy or compulsive?*

Your answers to the two questions below indicate how healthy your drive is.

- Do you love what you're doing?
- Do you get satisfaction out of most days?

George L. Ball is president and chief executive officer of Prudential-Bache Securities. During the week he usually puts in fourteen hours a day and as many as seven on weekends. How does he do it? "I work until it becomes work," he explains. "Then I stop. I enjoy my job a great deal—it's fun, it's invigorating, it's intellectually stimulating, and it's exciting. Success comes from that enjoyment, not from a mania about winning."

When you enjoy the day-to-day process of getting to your goal, you get satisfaction out of every day, not just the end result of your efforts. Ask yourself whether you really love what you're doing. If you truly care about your work, you won't risk burnout the way you might if you are solely interested in succeeding.

"One of the things that keep me able to go out there every day is that every day I truly love what I'm doing," says Rebecca Kelly. "I like to sweat and I like to get tired and I like to leap. I am wrapped up in living each day as it comes and I think that is a safe way to do it. I think the injuries and pressure come from people who are really putting all their energy into a goal that is large and not pacing themselves right."

3. Are you using your body's ability to relax to help you?

Many athletes know how to relax and breathe fully. They know that tension creates negative stress and injury, so they make a conscious effort to use what they know about their bodies to help them. Nothing averts disaster faster than taking a moment to breathe deeply and relax. Gather your forces, concentrate, and move powerfully, gracefully, and effortlessly ahead. That's how to finish the race.

Pay attention to what your body is telling you. If you feel tension in a muscle or limb, learn to relax it. Sports psychologists recommend systematically tensing and relaxing each muscle from your face down to your toes.

4. Are you honestly evaluating your goal and your progress toward it?

It helps occasionally to clear your head, to take a step back from your efforts and evaluate your situation. "If someone is really pushing on a specific project like making the team or getting an ad campaign done, they need to come back to reality and examine where they are," explains Dr. Jacobs. "How much have they achieved, how far do they have to go? You need to get yourself reoriented."

If you are in touch with your feelings about what you're doing, you should know and feel when burnout is coming.

"I don't believe I can burn out because I believe that I know when I'm going to reach my break-even point," says Vicky Aden. "I know what I want, and when I get it, I'll stop. When you pass your break-even point, then you burn."

5

The Finishing Syndrome

What keeps you going hour after hour when the obstacles look overwhelming and the rewards seem few? Where does the ability to reach deep into the gut and find the strength to go on—long after the body is spent—come from? How do you get past the phase when you want more than anything in the world to quit?

There comes a time in everyone's life when you have a clear but difficult choice: Do you press on against the obstacles and through the pain, or do you quit?

The "Should I Quit?" Question

Before you even begin to put your staying power to the test, you have to make sure you are using your energy wisely. Pushing yourself for the mere sake of proving you can push yourself will not be productive if circumstances (weather, timing, coworkers, boss) are not working in your favor, or if you lack the basic ability, talent, or technical skill necessary to accomplish the task at hand.

It's up to you to determine if circumstances and abilities are working in your favor. *What we are concerned with here is developing your mind-set so that you can be in the state of mind necessary to get the job done.* To determine how ready you are to face the challenge, answer yes or no to the following:

1. I feel inspired and motivated enough to take on this challenge.

2. I think my motives are healthy. I'm doing this for my own benefit, not to prove a point to someone else.

3. I have taken or will take steps to acquire the abilities I need to pursue this goal wisely and realistically.

4. I feel that I am in tune with my mind and body and that I am prepared to listen to them to monitor my progress.

5. Circumstances will not cause me to risk unnecessary injury, expense, time, or effort.

6. I believe I want this badly enough to push on despite setbacks, boredom, tedium, or flagging interest.

7. I feel able to take on mental and/or physical discomfort. My goal is worth it.

If you answered no to the majority of these statements, you are not ready to take on the project you have in mind. Examine each negative statement carefully.

- If the circumstances aren't in your favor, decide on a different tactic or arrange them so they are.
- If your talent or skill at the moment isn't up to par, commit yourself to doing more training and/or research.
- If you are not sure you are ready to handle discomfort, try a miniature version of your project. Use the trial run to test yourself, to see how it feels and how you respond.
- If your motives feel wrong, scratch the project. Try to analyze why you have a need to prove yourself. Be pleased that you caught your false motives at such an early stage before wasting time or energy.

Developing Mental Toughness

There is one thing that keeps you going, one trait that separates the finishers from the quitters—mental toughness. . It is the key to enduring anything. It's what the six-day runner has in common with the corporate executive who is working fourteen-hour days.

Everyone has the ability to keep going. It is a choice. You decide that you're going to see something through and then stick to that decision. *The decision to keep going is the mental effort that gets you through.*

Lawyer and ultra-marathoner Mike Frankfurt knows from experience that half the battle of pushing yourself through any long, tough event—like a fifty-mile race—is mental effort. "The first time I tried it, I had to quit after thirty-seven miles," says Frankfurt, who believes his decision to quit was based on both mental and physical condition. "When you run those races, you hit stages when you want to quit. It's really fifty percent psychological. If you push past that stage, you'll keep going. You have to decide before you start."

The same is true of any pursuit. Before you begin, make the decision to stick with what you're doing. That choice will help see you through. Eventually, perseverance becomes a way of life.

The Finishing Phases

To get through any endurance endeavor, it helps to know what to expect. What *do* we go through en route to our goal? There are a series of phases we pass through during any endurance effort. Expect the following chain of events:

1. The Fresh Start
2. The Work
    a. "Wanting to quit more than anything in the world"
    b. "Almost halfway there"
    c. The Twilight Hours
3. The Second Wind
4. After sheer exhaustion: quiet determination
5. The Final Kick

Being aware of these phases may help get you through them. Knowing that a rough spot is only a *phase* and will pass may be all you need to know to push on. These phases may vary from person to person. Some may reoccur or occur in a different order, or you might skip one altogether. Most athletes experience these phases during training sessions and endurance feats. In work situations we encounter them anytime we push ourselves—for example, working for ten hours straight or staying up overnight to meet a deadline. I've been through the phases hundreds of times, especially while swimming the English Channel for eighteen hours, while performing on Broadway for nearly two years, and while writing this book.

These phases constitute what I call the Finishing Syndrome. Using my English Channel swim as an example, let's go on a journey through the mind as it progresses through the Finishing Phases.

PHASE 1. THE FRESH START

When you first start out, the adrenaline created just by beginning carries you for a while. You feel fresh and strong, and the entire workout, race, or workday lies ahead like virgin territory.

As you warm up, wake up, and get the kinks out, you find your pace—establish your rhythm. You begin monitoring your stroke or cadence, get your thoughts in order, and settle in for the task that lies ahead.

While I'm swimming, I spend the first hour or so working through whatever is on my mind. I think about what I'm doing and how I feel. I contemplate what's to come. In the Channel the first few hours were sheer pleasure. I was delighted to be in the water, to have great weather, and to get my shot at France.

At the beginning of a workday, of a thirty-minute run, or at the start of a project, you may need a little push to get going. But once you've begun, you have made a commitment. It is with hope and energy that you move ahead.

PHASE 2. THE WORK

Somewhere down the road—four hours into a distance swim, eleven o'clock on a business day, ten minutes into a very intense half-hour Nautilus workout—the joy and freshness wear thin. It isn't the actual time involved—whether it's hours, months, or minutes—that takes us through these phases. It is the intensity of the effort and the involvement.

What began with high hopes and boundless energy has

become *work*. The end is nowhere in sight and you begin to wonder: What am I doing here? How did I get myself into this? Will I ever finish? How much longer will this go on? Commodities trader Vicky Aden admits that during particularly hectic, tense working days there are times when "I want to stop. Everything hurts. I ask myself why the hell I'm doing this anyway. I'm just coming in and out of the same office, talking to the same people, doing the same things."

The *work* hit me in the fourth hour of my Channel swim. *Everything* hurt—my shoulders, my wrists, my legs, my face. "This is *not* fun," I muttered. "This is the stupidest idea you have ever come up with." The self-abasement continued. I prayed for a respectable excuse to quit. A hurricane would have done nicely.

But the pain was not debilitating and my pride and self-worth were at stake. I figured the discomfort could not get any greater, and the level it was at was tolerable. So I pressed on. To my relief, the aches subsided within the hour, and I discovered it was merely a *phase*.

Since my first dramatic encounter with "wanting to quit more than anything in the world," I evolved some theories about the phenomenon. I discovered that "wanting to quit more than anything in the world," "almost halfway there," and the Twilight Hours were all parts of Phase 2, The Work. Getting through the Work phase may be tough—be it on a swim, a job, or in a relationship—but it divides the quitters from the finishers.

"Wanting to Quit More Than Anything in the World"

This feeling usually manifests itself as overall fatigue and/or pain, boredom, or depression. It is brought on by doing the same task repeatedly or mindlessly. You can be at the typewriter for hours and your brain gets cloudy and your fingers begin striking the wrong keys. You can go out with the same person for months and one day it occurs to you that you haven't exchanged any new or interesting ideas in a very long time. You can be performing the same show, eight times a week, week after week, and one night, mid-scene, get lost and wonder, "Have I said that line yet tonight, or was it last night?"

These sensations are not pleasant. They can be downright frightening. But it is only a *phase*. As quietly as it snuck up on you, it will fade away. The only way to save the relationship, finish the job, and keep that paycheck coming, is to *patiently endure*.

Likewise, during a physical endurance task, the bodily discomfort involved must also be endured. Some physiological depressions are predictable and may be triggered by mental depression or vice versa (see "Combating the Physiological Changes" later in this chapter).

"Almost Halfway There"

There is a low that hits as you approach the halfway point. You've got *more* than halfway yet to go. The road is still up, there's no rest in sight, and you're feeling too tired to imagine going farther than you've already gone.

On my eight-to-ten-hour swims the fourth and fifth hours are usually the toughest. I learned that most people who don't complete their Channel swims quit right about halfway. John Howard concedes that the fourth and fifth days of his ten-day Race Across AMerica were the hardest. One ultra-distance runner reports that he was in the most pain and wanted desperately to give up during the fortieth to sixtieth miles of his hundred-mile run.

When you get past halfway, there is less distance ahead than what you've left behind. You're over the mountain. The rest is the ride home.

The Twilight Hours

The "twilight hours" result from a physiological depression or low caused by a change in body temperature, a drop in blood sugar level, and/or sleep deprivation. I can actually feel my mind slipping into the twilight zone as my blood sugar drops and I start to feel the cold. I feel raw and vulnerable—very emotional. I usually get grim, quiet, unresponsive. I've worked with swimmers who get irritable and yell or throw things. Some get silly and act irrationally or irresponsibly. Some athletes break down and sob.

Athletes don't have a monopoly on the rawness that comes from sleep deprivation or low blood sugar. A doctor on call too many nights in a row, a mother kept up with a sick baby, a businessman cramming extra hours into an already busy schedule to meet deadline hit the Twilight Hours, too.

Combating the Physiological Changes

The physiological changes that bring on these emotional outbursts can be dealt with. By recognizing them once they occur, they can be countered. By predicting them *before* they occur and by being forewarned, they can sometimes be avoided.

A change in body temperature can be combated with the right food. On a cold swim take hot fluids. A little extra body fat (extra weight) will insulate against cold water. (See chapter 12 for details on hypothermia.) In a hot-weather running or biking race, drink plenty of cool (not cold) fluids.

The athlete who experiences a drop in blood sugar may need to take feedings with a higher glucose content and consume them more frequently. The secretary experiencing the drop in blood sugar that has her dozing at her desk can benefit from a feeding, too—some high-energy food like nuts, raisins, fruit, or juice.

As you run for six days, work into the early morning, or do anything that forces you to postpone sleep and continue working, you are dealing with sleep deprivation. It is not easy to beat. When drowsiness settles over the body and you can't stop to nap, there isn't much you can do. Start praying for your second, third, or twelfth wind.

Falling asleep during a long athletic endeavor can be a serious problem. Concentration fades and accidents can happen. When I start to doze off on a long swim, I keep stroking but less efficiently. I've almost crashed into my escort boat or slipped off into a deeper sleep state. Feedings help revive my energy. Ultimately, I have to force myself to concentrate, fight the sleep mentally, and just refuse to give in.

John Howard says that on a long bike ride, like the ten-day trek cross-country, he falls asleep and just stops pedaling. If he doesn't snap to in time, he falls over.

When the body is getting too tired to keep going and the concentration is fading dangerously, the fear produced by a near disaster may get the adrenaline pumping and keep you awake. Getting angry will get the adrenaline going, too. Some coaches yell at their athletes to get them angry and moving when everything else fails.

Athletes who have experienced all components of Phase 2 have personal bywords that help get them through. I find myself repeating these phrases during nonathletic pursuits as often as on the physical ones. For John Howard the phrase is "I can do this."

"I Can Do This"

John Howard hit bottom when he found out he was in last place during his first bicycle race across America. "I was ten hours down on the man [Lon Haldeman] that won. That's an impossible margin to make up." Catching up with

71

Lon would have given John the boost he needed to finish. He knew that if he could get to Lon, he could pass him. But he knew he'd never get to him. Still, he kept telling himself, "Just put your head down and go a little harder. A little more determination. I'm strong. I can do this. *I can do this.* You repeat that in your head a billion times before it's over."

John's determination pulled him up to second place with a time of 10 days, 10 hours, and 59 minutes—about 15 hours behind Haldeman. And he clocked the fastest first-time crossing of America, breaking Haldeman's first-time record by 12½ hours.

"Just Keep Going"

Cindy Nicholas, Queen of the English Channel, is asked what her "secret" is. How can she swim for so long? "There is no secret," she says. "You just keep going. Because if you stop, you're not going to make it."

The only thing you can be sure of is that if you *keep going,* whatever your speed, the finish *will get closer. Stopping doesn't get you anywhere.*

When you want to quit, you feel very much alone and that no one understands your pain and depression. But you are not alone. We all want to quit at some time or other. The difference between the people who stop and the people who don't is that when the people who quit hit that phase, they don't *think*, they just *quit*. The finishers keep talking to themselves, thinking things through. They figure it won't make any sense to stop while they're working it all out. And by the time they've finished thinking about it, the phase is over and they haven't quit. They're still in the race, or on the job, or in the relationship.

PHASE 3: THE SECOND WIND

Once you have endured the discomfort, the difficulties, and the hard work, and after the Work phase has passed, a new sensation takes over.

By the fifth hour of my Channel swim, all the aches and pains had subsided. That overwhelming fatigue didn't come over me again. Not only had the aches gone away but I felt *great*! Nothing and nobody was going to stop me. I felt that I could swim forever—if they flooded the sky, I could swim to the moon.

When the boredom and "Why am I here?" doubts fade, they are replaced with a whole new sense of creativity—a new approach. It's like starting fresh again, without the inexperience of the first time. It's better. It's exciting. It's kind of like falling in love with your mate again after being together for twenty years.

Dr. Laurie Solomon, M.D., talks about her "second wind" during her third year of medical school, when she was on call at the hospital every third or fourth night. She'd feel so tired that she'd want to go to sleep, but then she'd hit a new level and feel as though she could stay up another twenty-four hours. "There were times when I'd be up all night and I'd notice that I was exhausted but that I was running on something . . . I hesitate to use the term 'runner's high,' because it's different, there's a certain exhilaration with that. But there was this force inside that was propelling me to just go through all these actions, although you knew you were really tired."

PHASE 4. AFTER SHEER EXHAUSTION: QUIET DETERMINATION

By Phase 4 you are *beyond* depression, exhaustion, pain, and any number of second winds that have reenergized you. Quitting is no longer even an option. Something else takes over—*complete efficiency.* You haven't the energy to be anything less than completely efficient. And with that efficiency comes quiet determination.

The fourteenth hour of my Channel swim looked hopeless. For three hours I had swum against a strong current and had inched only one mile closer to France. The westerly tides running off the French shore made progress nearly impossible. It was getting dark and I felt cold.

From on board the escort boat, Dad told me that there was still a remote chance of getting into shore, but it would take six or seven more hours to cover the remaining five miles. I had been in mid-60° waters for more than half a day. The current was still against me. I was ready to go home and sleep. I wanted it to be finished already. I raised my goggles and said, "I'm tired. Let's go home." My support crew looked somber as they prepared the blankets and towels.

But something kept me from reaching out to touch the boat, which would have ended the swim immediately according to the Channel Swimming Association's rules. I refused to believe that a year of dreaming, preparing, and sacrificing could end short of my goal. I calmly treaded water, wishing for some miracle, as I waited for the final word from the boat pilot, Eric Baker.

"We're still five miles offshore, but we've navigated to three miles north of Cape Gris-Nez [a piece of land that juts two miles off the coast of France]. If you can swim *really* hard for one more hour, we still have an outside chance."

"Can you go on?" Dad asked.

One more hour? What's one more hour out of the rest of my life? Still a chance? Could I go on? From deep inside a spent and hungry swimming machine came a strong, determined voice. "Yes." *Yes,* I had another hour in me. It was not over yet.

74

I slowly made my way toward France, cutting in against the tide, as the hour stretched into four.

There were a hundred and one things that kept me going with quiet determination: I did not *want* to quit . . . I knew I would be home and asleep the next day, whether I made it or not . . . I was unwilling to give the people who had bet against me and who would gloat at my failure the satisfaction of collecting . . . I didn't want to train another whole year to come back and try again . . . I knew I couldn't afford to train another year and come back . . . I needed to get on with my life and new dreams and wanted to be satisfied with the way this dream turned out . . . I wanted to make my father—the man who'd turned gray watching and loving me all day from the deck of the ship—proud.

Physical ability had very little to do with it by that time. The struggle was acknowledged and accepted. There was nothing left to do but put my head down and get the job done.

PHASE 5. THE FINAL KICK

I was in my seventeenth hour in the Channel when everyone on board got very excited. Dad shouted, "Julie, we're only three-quarters of a mile off the point [Cape Gris-Nez]. Can you see it?"

I looked up. Through the dark and fog of my goggles I saw the lights of France. It was the first time all day that I had seen land. I *knew* then that I would make it. I *picked up my pace* and proceeded onward toward France with fresh energy.

At the end of a long haul, when the finish is finally in view, whatever energy you have left "kicks" in and you go for it. You've seen marathon runners *sprint* the final two hundred yards of a 26.2-mile race. You've found extra energy to get the job done as 5 P.M. approaches and you know you'll be going home soon. We've felt the final "kick" and wondered where this last burst of power comes from, when there shouldn't be anything left.

But we are remarkable pacing machines, capable of enduring whatever we have to, to get the job done. And when we have passed through all the phases, and finally finished, there is a hearty satisfaction in the proclamation "I did it!"

Suggestions to Help You Get Through the Five Phases

THINK POSITIVELY

Mind-set and mental outlook are all-important. If you think you're going to do well, you probably will. Don't let self-defeating thoughts get in your way. If you're worried about failing, you'll defeat yourself before you even begin. You'll also waste valuable effort that could be better spent progressing forward. *When you push yourself to the limit, you can't be worried about failing. You'll need your energy for the task at hand.*

The hallmark of the Rebecca Kelly Dance Company is a high-energy style and performers who are known to dance full out. According to Kelly, this is not happenstance. That's the way she trains her dancers.

At her studio she conducts classes and rehearsals in an environment where dancers are not worried about failing. "For those who know anything about the limit, it really is a wonderful experience," explains Rebecca. "I'm trying to get the dancers to crave that experience—to try their hardest and do their everything and give their all to something they believe in. There are many dancers who hold back lest they fail. I am trying to pull out the essence of their performing ability. I encourage them to feel addicted to performing and moving at their capacity. It's living more fully. It's like quenching your thirst."

DON'T LET OPPOSITION DISCOURAGE YOU

Besides fighting off all self-defeating thoughts from within, you might also be put into a position where you have to contend with opposition from other people. It's always helpful when you have some support from friends, parents, a mate. But you can't always rely on others, especially if you know more about what you are doing than they do. Stick to your project. You know better than anyone else how much you want to achieve your goal and how capable you are of getting there. Take into account who is discouraging your effort. Try to figure out why.

GO AHEAD AND CRY—IT CAN HELP

Some individuals need to take a little time to break down in order to keep on going. Once they let their feelings out, it's easier for them to continue.

"I was in agony," says Stu Mittleman of one of his six-day runs. "I went through a period when I didn't want to be there. It was the most intense extension of the feeling 'I don't want to be here.' I wanted to give it up. But that's one thing about six-day races: Ten hours later the race is still going on and you might want to continue.

"There was a moment when I did break down. I started crying. Ray [his trainer] was in the tent and I was holding him. He was holding me and I was crying. He said, 'Get yourself together, go out there and run the next thirty-six hours and you'll get your five hundred miles and you'll never have to do another of these things again.'

"Without a moment's hesitation, I said, 'I am going to run another one of these things. I'm just not happy *now*. But it's not because I've given up.'

"I broke because I realized I wasn't going to have the race at that moment, that it was someone else's. I'd worked hard for it. This was my way of getting it out. I went back out and ran the next thirty-six hours."

Stu finished the race seventh out of thirty runners and feels he had an "honorable, historic, admirable run."

GET TO KNOW WHAT IT FEELS LIKE WHEN EVERYTHING "CLICKS" AND NOTHING IN THE WORLD COULD MAKE YOU WANT TO QUIT.

Finishing isn't *always* like fighting and winning a major war. Once in a while, the event goes exactly as planned, without a hitch, and with tremendous satisfaction.

When I swam twice around Manhattan, I was more prepared than I had ever been for anything in my life. I looked forward to the day, felt ready, and just wanted to do it. There was never a time during the swim when I thought I couldn't make it or worried that my training hadn't been adequate. I admit I felt chilled in the night, got a little drowsy, and was nearly run down by a press boat while making my way up the East River for the finish, but for the most part, I enjoyed the swim—all 21 hours, 2 minutes, and 49 seconds of it. Finishing was simply doing what I had planned.

When John Howard set the world record in May 1983 for the most number of miles biked in twenty-four hours (514), he felt the same way. "I was in shape. I'd trained well for it," John recalls. "I was ready. It was just a matter of doing it. Everything clicked."

There are times when you *are* well prepared for the task

before you and nothing—not even unforeseen obstacles—can stand in your way. John Howard didn't let seven flats or the hours of rain (eighteen out of twenty-four) stand in his way. He was able to change each tire and still stay far enough ahead of the time he needed on each lap to gain his record.

Mike Frankfurt also knows how it feels when all the pieces—whether it's training for a race or preparing a case—fall properly into place. "There are times when everything works perfectly," says Mike. "Your time [in running] is better than it's ever been. It's the same thing when you close or make a deal or help someone to set up, buy, or sell a business. *Everything* just works and you get that great feeling."

The greater the obstacles along the way, the harder the road, and the more desperately you wanted to quit—the sweeter the taste of finishing. There is tremendous joy there. It is a land of determination, of conquering, of challenge. It is a land worth visiting.

6

Not Finishing: Learning from It and Living with It

Sometimes it's a breeze, sometimes it's hard, sometimes it's *very* hard, and once in a while you fail. Not everyone finishes the job he or she begins. For every inspiring story of courage and strength, there must be hundreds that end differently. How do you deal with not finishing? Is not finishing the same as failure?

When you're devoted to your project and putting out a great deal of energy, stopping short of your goal seems like failing. It can make you feel guilty, angry, hurt, dismayed, and let down. Giving up can cause as much emotional anguish as staying on—maybe more.

But sometimes giving up is healthy. There are instances when not finishing is *not* failure, when the weather or the odds are unpreventably against you or when pushing on could result in injury or burnout. There are times when admitting you are exhausted, sick, or in above your head is the *wise* choice.

Quitting—a Learning Experience

Quitting isn't always a loss. Sometimes it can be a learning experience. In every champion's career there comes a time when you decide whether you've gone as far as you can or want to go. You make a choice to stop. Not finishing can be a positive step forward when you gain self-knowledge about your abilities and your goals. Quitting becomes a learning experience if you use a loss as a stepping stone to greater victory in the future; if you learn from your mistakes and prevent them from happening the next time around; and if you admit failure and mature by learning to live with it.

Keep Failure in Perspective

Choreographer Rebecca Kelly keeps the possibility of failure in perspective. "If I go to the limit and fail, I will have had the satisfaction of knowing I tried my hardest," explains Rebecca. "I'm not afraid as I was when I was younger to fail. You don't die from failure and it doesn't mean you're a bad person. It just might reveal something to you about your goals that you have to change."

Swimmer Cindy Nicholas can top her list of accomplishments with the title "Queen of the English Channel," which she received after completing nineteen crossings. The only times Cindy ever got out of the water without finishing what she set out to do were the two times when she attempted a triple crossing—and she didn't stop the swims until she had completed two and one-third of the three crossings. Nevertheless, the Canadian press reported that she had *failed* at these attempts at the triple. Cindy, on the other hand, knew that these swims were her best efforts and accepted what she had been able to complete.

On Cindy's first attempt at the triple, she swam two laps and started back for the third, when bad weather made it impossible to continue. She tried again less than two weeks later. Again, she completed a double crossing and was one-third of the way back when she stopped. This time she got out because she was physically exhausted.

"I knew I had really pushed myself beyond my limit and I amazed myself that I had gotten that far," says Cindy. "Physically, I was falling asleep. It was a combination of being hypothermic and just exhausted. I was disappointed, but very excited that I had gone as long as I did. If I had to choose one swim where I really worked until I couldn't work anymore, that would be it. Usually I feel at the end of a swim that I could've given a bit more. But this time I felt that I couldn't have gone anymore. I was really quite proud of myself, even though I didn't do what I had set out to do. It was a feeling that I hadn't mentally given up—I just physically couldn't do anymore. The last twenty-two hours was pain the whole way and I was really surprised that I could go that long. You can't be disappointed in yourself; you're really disappointed in the circumstances. That's why not making the three-way has never been a crushing defeat for me, because I really did try so hard."

Learning from Your Mistakes in Order to Prevent Them

To learn about what happened, play over the entire process in your mind, beginning with setting the goal.

Assess how far you've gotten and the factors that didn't allow you to succeed. Once you've learned what got in the way of your success, you'll be able to plan an improved strategy for the next undertaking.

SET REALISTIC GOALS

Setting realistic goals can save a lot of wear and tear on the body and keep the ego from getting too severely bruised. For John Howard it wasn't weather, exhaustion, or pain that made him quit the 1983 Nevada City bike race. Reassessing his position, he realized that he just hadn't the "right stuff." John had won the race in 1969. When he got an invitation to enter the race in 1983, he was nostalgic. Even though he would be the oldest competitor by ten years, he figured he could beat the other guys.

John admits that it was "a race which I never should have entered, because I wasn't ready for it. I kind of let my ego get into the picture. Forget it. My focus was wrong. I had been doing triathlons. I hadn't been doing enough speed work, hadn't been putting in enough miles. I was too heavy. I could go on and on. But I just let all that stuff sort of slide away. 'I can do it,' I told myself. 'I'm great.' So I did the race and I bombed. I wasn't competitive. That is, I didn't have it.

"I quit the race. It was embarrassing. It was a grave disappointment, followed by realistic expectations instead of these wild sensations that I could do anything I chose to do."

Accept Responsibility
for Your Actions

Taking responsibility for your actions can help you to conduct honest self-evaluation, accept and assert control over your own life, and understand your strengths and weaknesses so you'll be better prepared for the next project.

It's easy to blame someone or something for your failure. And it hurts a lot less, too. But shirking the responsibility for what's happened won't teach you anything about yourself or about the experience you've just come through.

Commodity trader Vicky Aden does a "mental marathon" every day. Her successes and failures are demonstrated for everyone to see—every day. "A sheet of paper is generated daily that says how much money I've made the prior day," explains Vicky. "Every single solitary day. I can't hide that."

In her business Vicky believes it is impossible to hide any laziness, mistakes, or lack of knowledge. "Everything ends up back on the floor and everything is counted in dollars and cents. You cannot hide your dirty laundry, because every day it's counted."

From her everyday successes and failures, Vicky has learned that "the market has no mercy. You make a decision and you have to live by it. Even if you don't make a decision, you've made a decision. You either buy, sell, or don't do either. After living with the market for a while, you begin to accept your responsibility and your choice. You are responsible about making a choice and accepting the consequences of it."

Vicky has found that although it might be easy to hide the truth from yourself, it's impossible to be physically evasive with yourself, especially when the facts, in dollars and cents, face you every day.

Through the years John Howard has learned to assume responsibility for whatever happens to him in a race. In the 1983 Hawaii Ironman triathlon he was a victim of the famed tack attack: An unhappy bystander littered the bike course with carpet tacks, creating a great number of blowouts and frustrated bikers. John got two flats and was out of the race because he didn't have any more spares. However, he takes responsibility for his misfortune, claiming he could have prevented it. "I could have kept my head up, watched, seen," he explains. "You puncture because you're not as aware as you should be. I will ride my bike at night without lights and steer between potholes. You make your luck."

Admit Failure and Learn to Live with It

If you're able to analyze the factors that made you give up, you can learn a great deal about yourself. You might find out you don't *always* have it in you, and there's nothing wrong with that.

Stu Mittleman's name was synonymous with the hundred-mile race. He had won the National Championship in 1980, 1981, and 1982. In 1983 he entered the race and did the unthinkable—he dropped out.

"I hurt and was beginning to be in agony," he recalls. "The whole enterprise seemed not worth it. I had reached a point where it seemed more productive—more wild—to stop. I wasn't convinced that I would leave that thing feeling good about myself and I wasn't convinced that to continue on wouldn't lead to a serious injury. My groin hurt. Then I got hit by a bicycle and it just seemed like such an absurdity.

"I dropped out when I finally convinced myself that I had done everything I could to prepare for the race, I was proud of what I had done as a runner, and I could live with myself without winning the race. I had entered so many of these things before and this was the worst I had ever felt and, at that point, I felt that if I pushed myself through it, I might not enjoy doing another one later on."

So Stu quit. He reasoned it through, believing he could live with the decision. "I walked away from that race, and for the first time in my adult life, I realized that I didn't need to be a champion to be happy with myself. I could walk away from ultra-distance running at any moment, and that was important for me to know.

"I wasn't sure whether I was running *away* from things or running *to* things. Most people assumed that I was running away from things, that I was unhappy, that I was prolonging childhood, that I was refusing to become an adult. And I was unsure. But when this thing happened and I realized I wasn't upset, I wasn't blaming someone else for my disappointments, because I *was* disappointed, that was important for me to know."

Walking away from the race did not negatively influence later performances. In fact, two weeks later, Stu ran his first six-day race, finished second overall, and set a new American record for the greatest number of miles—488 miles and 96 yards—run in six days.

Failure Can Be Used as a Stepping Stone

Some people react to defeat by gearing up for the next challenge. They use their feelings of loss, anger, or frustration to push them on. They are determined not to let one failure keep them down.

One woman I know was caught up in a political squabble and fired from her job at an architectural firm. She had done well at school and had never really "failed" at anything. So everyone assumed that being unemployed would make her upset and desperate. She was very angry about the way she'd been treated. But she didn't let her anger destroy her; instead she used it positively. She was determined that she would show the people who had fired her who she was and what she could do. She set off and started her own now-successful company.

Not Finishing: Learning from It and Living with It

For some athletes, not finishing one event gives them the push to excel in the next one. Bill Schmidt debuted on the world professional marathon swimming circuit in July 1984. The first race was 22.5 miles around Atlantic City. The field was strong, but Schmidt was fresh off the 1984 Olympic trials and he was fast. Rumor had it that he could beat the champion, Paul Asmuth. Says Bill, "I knew I was in good shape. I really thought I could win. Or at least come in second."

The race began and the water was a lot colder than Bill expected; it's usually in the seventies, but this day it was in the low sixties. Not far along, a heavy fog rolled in, making visibility extremely poor at best. And the water temperature began to drop. Some reports claimed it was as low as 50°.

As Schmidt got colder, his skin turned gray, his senses became dulled, and he stopped making progress. "I thought he was going to die," said his brother Rob, who was on the escort boat. "Bill was starting to act like a two-year-old. I'd ask, 'Are you okay?' But he couldn't even talk. Then I told him to start swimming. He just couldn't. So I told him to give me his hand—he couldn't. The crew and I pulled him out."

Bill was taken to the hospital and treated for hypothermia. He recovered within hours. "I was kind of embarrassed," he recalls. "Here I was, fresh off the Olympic trials, and a lot of people had thought I could win. I was enjoying the attention they were paying me before the race. . . . Then I didn't even finish." He decided, at first, not to go to the next race in Magog, Quebec.

But the fact that twelve out of nineteen swimmers didn't finish the Atlantic City race showed that he was not alone. Eventually, he let himself get talked into going on. "The other swimmers assured me it wouldn't be that cold. And I really wanted to prove that I could complete it. I knew I was in good enough shape."

So he reevaluated his goals. At Atlantic City he'd gone in to win. For this race his goal was "just to finish. I needed to finish." The water was warmer, in the mid-seventies, and Bill swam in first or second place all day. When he emerged first out of the water, *winning* the race, he said, "I knew I had a performance like that in me, but I just wasn't sure after last week in Atlantic City."

With his confidence renewed he went on to the next race in Lac-Saint-Jean, Quebec. When he trained in the water during the week, he couldn't stay in for more than a half hour, it was so cold. But "it's warmer than Atlantic City," he told himself. "I think I can make it."

From the moment he hit the water on race day, he was freezing. "I lost my breath, I was so cold. My legs were tight from shaking." He was in such pain that he couldn't kick at all.

Bill finished in twelfth place and was "*very, very* satisfied. What made me feel best was people coming up to me, the other swimmers, and saying, 'You stuck in there . . . you really showed guts . . . you were tough as nails all day.' I felt great."

Was not finishing one race a failure? Bill suffered hypothermia in the Atlantic City race and, painful though it was for his brother, the decision to pull him out was the wise one. That first race led Bill on to two personal victories.

Unattained Goals

Everyone has some unfulfilled dream, some unresolved business. Some, like John Howard, Stu Mittleman, Cindy Nicholas, and Bill Schmidt, have accepted not finishing and have grown from the experience. Deep in their hearts, they may wish things had ended differently, but they don't let what happened get in their way. The defeats, large or small, are steps toward greater victories.

It can be sad or painful when things are left undone or are out of reach, as happens in an unresolved relationship or by the death of someone close to you. You know you will never see or hold that person again, but you go on with your life.

When I was a kid, I wanted to be *lots* of things when I grew up—an actress on Broadway, a lawyer, a teacher, a veterinarian, an Olympic athlete. . . . Some of these dreams faded into passing fancies. Others I pursued with intensity. One of my father's friends once asked me why I had chosen to study acting in college. "It's so hard to earn a living in theater. Why not pick something more *practical*?"

"I may not be any good," I told him. "But I have to find that out. I think the saddest two words are 'if only.' Twenty years from now I *refuse* to look back and say, 'What would have happened *if* I'd tried to be an actress? If only I'd given it a chance when my whole life was ahead of me.' "

I know many people who have fulfilled some of their dreams but still have others they've never pursued: the successful businesswoman who wants to bike across America before she's forty . . . the best-selling novelist who wants to be a film star . . . the mother of three who wants to go back to school for a master's degree. Years go by and their desires nag at them. Pursuing their dreams and attaining them would change their lives. But they don't go after them because they can't leave the business or have to wait until the children are grown or the odds are against them.

They never even begin—or they start and give up ("I didn't have the time . . . I'm too old . . . I didn't have the money"). They accept their own excuses and suppress the knowledge that it *wasn't* time or age or money that kept them from their goal—it was their own lack of desire, lack of talent, or fear of risk and not winning.

As much as I dreamed of competing in the Olympics and still cry from some gut level when I watch great athletes earn their golds, I accepted at an early age that I was simply *not good enough* to compete on that level. So when I dreamed of swimming the English Channel, it was a re-creation of that Olympic goal. And when I stood on the shores of France, I had earned my gold. In some indirect way my childhood dream had been fulfilled.

It may hurt to press on through the pain or the depression. The sacrifices may be great. But I do not want to die wondering, "What if?" We each *deserve* our own version of the gold. You can't *always* get what you want, but you can *always* give it your best shot. That *effort*—when it's the most you can give—is something worth living for, whether you finish or not.

When Finishing Is More than a Game

In sports and in most things you have a choice: You can get out of the water, stop running, call off the game, miss your deadline, flunk the course. Quitting may not be particularly enjoyable or desirable, but it won't kill you.

However, there are a lot of instances when you don't have a choice. As one mother I know says about raising her two children, "There's no end to my race."

The same goes for a woman who is going through labor for nine hours. She may want desperately to stop the pain, to take a break, to forget the whole thing and not have her baby. But she can't. The baby must come. The farmer must harvest the crop before the frost kills it. He may have worked several days around the clock, feel wretched and exhausted, but he must keep working or the crops will die and his family will starve. The surgeon may be bleary-eyed after hours at the operating table, aching under the bright lights and the pressure of high-precision work, but he can't take time out. His patient depends on him. The choice is quit and die or keep going and survive. The strong survive.

What seems like failure or a setback is often a necessary phase toward progress. It's like walking upstairs, where each step is slightly bigger than the one before and more difficult to climb. Sometimes you trip and fall down a few. But the staircase ahead is the same staircase. It's all part of the learning process. You have to fail sometimes to know what your limits are, to know how far you can fall back, to know you can get through the disappointments and go on.

7

After Success/Post-Event Depression

You've pushed back your limits and reached your goal. You feel elated. Unfortunately, your joy doesn't last for long. It is interrupted by probing questions like "What's next?" and "What do I do now?" The questions rock you and you begin to feel unsettled, restless, empty, maybe even depressed. You miss your project, the goal, the struggle that kept you busy and on edge. How do you handle the letdown after a success?

After "I Did It"

When I crawled out of the East River after completing the first successful swim twice around Manhattan, I climbed up a rusty ladder, gingerly hauled my weary body over a steel-spiked fence, and nearly fell into my mother's arms. I was flooded with questions and accosted by cameras and microphones. When the "How do you feel?" . . . "What was it like?" . . . "What did you learn about yourself and our rivers?" questions were over, someone asked, "What's next?"

"What's next?" I echoed silently. Didn't I just do something? Wasn't that enough? You mean I have to do something *more*? I had just completed a year's work. I was floating on the high of success. I deserved to feel ecstatic. But, pow, right between the eyes came, "What's *next*?"

What is next? What comes *after* the great feat? Where does the first man to fly to the moon go *next*? How does the athlete top his Olympic gold, the playwright surpass her Pulitzer Prize, the mountain climber outclimb Mount Everest? It is extraordinarily hard to continually top yourself. It had been hard enough for me to find one thing in the world to be first to do. The pressure to find another, even greater thing was enormous. Must a successful feat be *sequeled*?

Feeling the Loss

A lot of time, preparation, sweat, and love is behind any major accomplishment—a long-distance swim, finishing a doctoral thesis, or starting up a company.

For each of my swims I have spent entire months preparing and sacrificing for one thing—a successful swim. The adventures were wonderful, the travel exciting, the people inspiring. Eventually, I achieved what I set out to do. I had spent a very focused segment of time in pursuit of a dream.

Although the process of reaching the goal was long, lonely, and sometimes unrewarding, I had grown to love the *pursuit*—the process, the journey, the effort—of achieving the goal. When the goal was reached, there was a sadness and a sense of loss. The *process* became the goal, and the actual goal represented an end to the process. As with a hunter, "at the moment of the kill, he feels regret, because in such ardent pursuit he must identify with his victim and so feel loss when the concentration of his effort dies," says David Smith, an adventurer, in *The Healing Journey*.

When the dream was won, I was lost. I was told that there would be a letdown when it was over. I felt prepared to face it. But it was more devastating than I had anticipated. The initial elation wears off sooner or later, the body recovers, and the "I did it" fades.

"I remember when I went to an award presentation and was on television for the first time," says Cindy Nicholas. "It was a great evening. The next day, I got home and I was so lost, coming down after a big, exciting event. One day I felt so important and the next day I was at home vacuuming. You have such enthusiasm and concentration for one thing that when it finishes, it's a letdown."

Six Suggestions for Coping with Post-Event Depression

1. Recognize that depression is a natural part of life's cycle.

Life is a series of ups and downs, good and bad feelings, ecstasies and lows. Often the letdown is inevitable; it is part of the process of putting out effort, succeeding, and taking up a new challenge.

Mike Frankfurt decided to practice communications and entertainment law because it was exciting to meet and work with creative people. Even though his field continuously challenges him, he finds that post-event depression is impossible to get away from.

"You could be on a hot streak, doing terrific things," he explains. "You finish a major deal and you accomplish something and the next day you're coming in and doing a lot of mundane things—which we all have to do. Then you go through a couple of days where there's nothing going on and you think, 'I'll never get another client again. This is the most boring thing I've ever done.' You do things that are exciting and satisfying, but not every day."

2. Recognize that the letdown you feel is your body's reaction to pushing yourself.

John Howard has observed that many triathletes go through a depression after an event. "I was talking to some triathletes after a race in Austin, Minnesota, and I could sense that they were a little down, a little depressed. I think it's a normal condition."

You don't feel the urge to go right back to intensive training, and to John Howard, that also is natural. "The body is telling you to back off. You don't have to stop training, but you should taper down considerably and do something else, some training that is fun or enjoyable. Try to do something physical, stay active. I think that's what the body needs."

Remind yourself that the depression won't last forever. Accepting it is one of the fastest ways of getting past it.

3. Foresee the depression and look beyond it to other goals.

Before you have finished your project, take a moment to think about the future. Just having several ideas about what you want to do next will help you to line up the next goal.

Life is a process. If you were ever finished striving, you'd be finished altogether.

"Unless you have something else to replace it—not necessarily another swim, but something that's really on your mind—it can be a big letdown," says Cindy Nicholas. "The letdown is not from the swim itself, but from the fact that you don't have another goal."

John Howard counsels athletes to plan goals for their entire season so that when one event is completed they have another to look forward to. "You should have a pattern with goals in the horizon for you," says John. "My theory on setting goals is to have short-term and then long-term goals. Everything you do is building up for the next event, part of the process."

4. Let go of the project and try to separate yourself from it.

Separating yourself from what you've done is hard to do, but it can be healthy and helpful in getting you out of a post-event slump.

It's difficult to let go of a success. The urge is to hold on to it and wrap yourself in its glory for as long as possible. But people who have been through post-event depression several times develop a maturity about their achievements and know when it is time to let go and turn to the next project.

Throughout an athletic or business career, you begin to realize that you, as an individual, exist outside of your work. When the project or athletic event is over, imagine it as being next to you, but not part of you. If you are unable to separate yourself, your identity will remain wrapped up in the project. That can be especially unhealthy and harmful, since when the event is over, you won't know what to do with yourself.

The process of separating is never easy. "You put everything into it [the project], all that effort, and then it's gone," notes Rebecca Kelly. "It must be like a baby you're connected to, like a cord attached to a product. I have to remember that no matter how much of my heart or soul I've put into a piece, it's not me, it's an abstraction, a thing outside me."

5. Time away from the project brings a healthy perspective to what you've done.

Stu Mittleman has been through enough events to know that his overall career as an athlete transcends each and every race. But he came to that decision after many successes, some failures, and above all, learning to deal with his own feelings after each event. Years of experience have allowed him to come to an understanding of what he does best.

"At one time I thought each one [event] was so important and I'd focus so much on it that when it was over it was hard to get back to anything else," explains Stu. "I think as time has gone on, each individual race in the overall scheme of things is less and less important. Now my life transcends any event, and an event is just a moment now."

6. If you see each goal as part of a lifetime process, you can build on each success.

Find what is positive about the project that's completed and use that in working toward future goals.

- What skills have you perfected?
- What have you learned?
- What aspects of your character can you now rely on?
- Do you now know more about the kinds of goals you want to set?

97

From her long-distance swimming career, Cindy Nicholas learned that feeling satisfied with herself had to be an essential part of any new endeavor. Swimming "has changed my life in different ways at different times," says Cindy. "There is a feeling now that I have to be doing something that satisfies me—not physically, but mentally. I always want to be learning, improving, using all my potential. Endurance is pushing yourself to the limit, pushing yourself beyond what you could be doing. This has always made me want to do better than I have been doing."

For Cindy "swimming the Channel was meaningful," and she wants always to feel as though she is doing something meaningful. Cindy is now a lawyer and she is approaching her career with the same brand of enthusiasm, discipline, and effort she used when swimming. "Becoming a lawyer became a swim in a way," she concludes.

Life Goes On— One Goal Replaces Another

Think of the mother who has just had a baby. Another life was literally part of her for nine months. Her thoughts and actions have been focused singularly on its well-being. She has abstained from alcohol and cigarettes, prayed for the child's health, feared birth defects. Finally, she gives birth. The baby is separate and apart. A void exists where warm life once was. The anticipation and worry are over. Postpartum depression sets in.

But the mother's feelings of emptiness and depression are replaced by lifelong goals—the growth, nurturing, and development of this baby. The process that was a special part of her life for nine months goes on—as does life after any major accomplishment.

Life becomes a series of goals and processes leading up

to each new goal. Each one will not necessarily surpass the one that came before, and some will not be successes. But they will forever be part of an ongoing, never-ending cycle: setting a goal, participating, finishing, feeling elation, depression . . . and moving forward again.

PART II

The Body

8

The High-Energy Endurance Life-Style

Athletes and business people who live high-energy life-styles know how to harness and use their energy. Full-time endurance athletes focus their entire lives on putting out maximum effort. In order to get more mileage, active people lead their lives in healthy, effective ways. To get where they are going, these people incorporate endurance into every aspect of their life-styles by taking care of their bodies as well as eating and sleeping for maximum output.

If you wanted your car or a piece of machinery to last a long time and to function well, you would take good care of it. The same goes for your body, the piece of machinery that carries you through life. Because athletes work with their bodies, they must pay extra attention to their physical well-being. But the principle stands for anyone. *If you want to go the distance or if you want to push yourself in any area of life, you'll want a body that can go with you, a body that can help you to enhance your mental endurance capabilities.*

Where does the energy for a high-energy life-style come from? What is the secret to high energy? Below, the keys to a high-energy life-style:

Energy begets energy.

How much do you expect of yourself? The more you expect of yourself, the more you can accomplish. If you believe that you only have enough energy to work from nine to five, then you will fulfill that belief. You'll feel tired and you won't have the energy to go to that evening class.

"The very act of being energetic is invigorating and creates even more energy," says George L. Ball, president and chief executive officer of Prudential-Bache Securities in New York City. "Investing energy and effort into a day encourages, enables, and makes it easier to expand the process. Put another way, the more you do, the greater your capacity to do well. That enhancement in and of itself is rewarding. Not being energetic would be tiring."

High-energy people have an unending interest in what they're doing.

If you love what you are doing, you won't notice the time pass. The pleasure you feel will give you boundless energy. "I think that if you are profoundly interested in what you are doing, then there is no such thing as fatigue," says Rebecca Kelly. "I feel that what happens is people get involved in things they're not committed to, then wonder why they don't have the energy or stamina to complete tasks or have extra time and energy for other things. I find that I'm one of the lucky people. We're people who are fulfilled, doing what we truly want to do. You find what you're meant to do and you do it, you give it your all. If you find it [what your work is], then you discover within yourself boundless energy to accomplish whatever it is you're doing."

High-energy people cut out excesses that waste time.

Some hardworking, successful people don't spend much time entertaining or socializing. They have trimmed down their lives to cut out excesses that, in the end, interfere and take them farther away from their goals.

J. Peter Grace is often in the news. He is not only chairman of W. R. Grace & Company but was also handpicked by President Ronald Reagan as the businessman who could head the Private Sector Survey on Cost Control, a group designed to suggest ways for the federal government to save money. He is seventy-two years old and sometimes clocks in eighteen-hour working days.

Grace's forte is cutting down on waste, so it's no coincidence that his life-style should exemplify ways of getting rid of waste in a hectic day. In a June 1984 article in *Management Accounting,* he explains how he handles one of the biggest executive problems—balancing home and work. "To be a very hard-hitting, hard-driving executive with businesses in 43 countries and still give time to your family is [terribly difficult]. The only solution we had was that I don't drink, we never entertain, we never go out."

It's not to say that successful people don't have fun, just that they have learned to prioritize.

Setting Up Your Own
High-Energy Regimen

Pushing yourself to the limit should be a process involving both the mind and the body. Neglect either area and the process of getting where you're going will be slowed down.

Enhancing all facets of your life with endurance is a holistic approach to living. Stu Mittleman's philosophy about running is an example of this holistic approach. Apply it to your life-style no matter what goal you are pursuing.

Stu believes that *just doing more*—in his case, increasing mileage—is not wise without taking other factors into consideration. When he increases his distance in preparation for a six-day or a hundred-mile race, he takes on other responsibilities at the same time because he doesn't see running as just running. "If you make the commitment to be a runner," says Stu, "that commitment carries with it other responsibilities besides putting in miles. If you look at it as just putting in miles, the likelihood is that you will break down." Stu divides his training into five integral parts: flexibility, strength, cardiovascular training, rest/recovery, and nutrition.

A high-energy life-style requires the same kind of overall attention to each part of your life: physical exercise, eating, and sleeping and rest.

To set up your own high-energy regimen, borrow the essential ingredients from the ultra-athletes and incorporate them into your own life.

PHYSICAL EXERCISE

Most ultra-athletes reap mental and physical benefits from exercise, especially since, for many of them, it is their life's work. By now, it has been proclaimed, publicized, touted, shouted, and screamed: *Physical exercise enhances the quality of anyone's life*. Exercise helps to make people healthy, both physically and mentally. It's used as therapy, for fun, as a mood lifter, for health. It also increases daily energy. Not to mention that pushing back your physical limits will help you to find out that your potential is limitless. Here is an example:

"I think running distance helped me in a lot of ways," explains Saul Schoenberg, vice-president of a major sports agency who has run in two New York City marathons. "I'm more relaxed. I think that the busier I am, the more I seem to accomplish. I rarely find that I'm too busy to get something done, even the extra things. You juggle things around, do things efficiently. Running has shown me that. I was able to run and get my marathon training in—fifty miles a week or better—and put in long working days as well, traveling all the time."

You'll find that fitting exercise into your life-style is well worth the effort. To start your own exercise program if you don't have one, or to increase your distance, see the next chapter.

EATING FOR ENERGY

Most ultra-athletes know what kinds of food give them high-performance abilities. For them the correlation between what they eat and how they feel and perform is easy to see. For them food is fuel. It is for you, too, whether you work behind a desk or stand up all day waiting on customers.

What do athletes know about fuel that can help you maintain a higher level of energy?

During a workout athletes can feel the fuel working

inside their bodies. They have energy highs and lows. Most often it is related to their diet. In a typical working day you, too, have energy slumps and energy highs and these can also be caused by the foods you eat. Each person's energy expenditure is different, and the amount of calories you need depends on how active you are and how quickly or slowly your metabolism works. The energy value of what you eat has more to do with the specific foods you select than with how much you eat.

Like the athlete who organizes his diet around the requirements of a race, you need to eat to maintain energy for a working day. You need foods that will get you going in the morning, keep you moving during the day, and wind you down in the evening before bed.

Most ultra-athletes eat whole, unrefined foods. They cut out additives, chemicals, and refined foods like white flour, sugar, white rice. They eat lots of complex carbohydrates, fruits, and vegetables.

Once you understand how the two main sources of fuel—fats and carbohydrates—are used in the body (the role of protein is to build and repair tissue), you can make intelligent decisions about what you eat based on getting those foods.

Fat has nine calories per gram, whereas carbohydrate has four. Fat is not an efficient fuel in the body because the nutrient takes awhile to be digested and absorbed. It deposits itself easily in fatty tissue. Research has shown that excess fat in the diet may have harmful cardiovascular effects.

Carbohydrates, on the other hand, are a cleaner, more efficient fuel, since they are easily digested and absorbed into the bloodstream. Note, however, that there are two types of carbohydrates—simple and complex. Complex carbohydrates—grains, legumes, vegetables—have a high nutritional value. Beans or bran, for example, are also high in fiber, which aids in the functioning of a healthy intestinal tract. Simple carbohydrates, such as fruits, are also nutritious. Beware, however: Refined sugars such as pastry or table sugar are also simple carbohydrates, but they lack nutritional value.

For a healthful, high-energy diet, cut back on dietary fats and refined sugars. Eat a moderate-protein, high-complex-carbohydrate diet.

Many dietary habits—skipping breakfast, eating a light lunch, and then consuming a three-course dinner—are not conducive to a day that requires high energy. Alter your eating habits to get more fuel from your meals. "Just as you change your life-style to accommodate exercise, you change your eating style," explains Steven Lichtman, director of the exercise physiology program at New York University's Department of Recreation. "If you change your eating patterns radically, you won't be able to sustain the changes. Do it gradually and incorporate them into your life-style."

Breakfast

The first meal of the day should get you through the morning. A breakfast that is high in fats and sugars—pancakes and syrup, doughnuts and coffee—will give you a temporary boost of energy but will make you feel tired later. Get some complex carbohydrates (whole-grain cereals and breads and fruits) as well as some protein (cheese) and a little bit of fat (a spoonful of peanut butter) into your breakfast.

Lunch

Get additional fuel at lunchtime with more complex carbohydrate foods and, again, a low amount of fat. Try vegetable platters, baked potatoes, or pasta. Be wary of heavy, high-fat meals that take awhile to digest. They can drain you of that much-needed afternoon energy surge and make you feel sluggish and tired when you need to be alert.

Dinner

Many nutritionists maintain that dinner should be the lightest meal of the day because you are winding down from the day's activities and don't need as much energy right before going to bed. Rich foods eaten late in the evening are bound to be deposited as fat.

REST AND SLEEP

Your body needs rest and recovery as much as it needs to be pushed. As businessman P. J. Johnson says, "You can't keep going all the time. You've got to get away and recharge. You've got to go to bed at night, put your head on the pillow, and say, 'I've done everything I possibly can today. I can't do anymore.'"

Putting in a full day can enhance the quality of your sleep. You'll feel physically and mentally worn out, and slightly drained from efforts expended during the day. That lovely feeling of weariness will put you right to sleep.

Just *knowing* that your body needs rest and relaxation can help you get the rest you need. "I've gotten to the point where I am not hung up on hours and hours of training," explains triathlete Lyn Brooks. "It's allowed me to relax and get more rest. There are now times where I have scheduled total days off. It's not just waking up and bagging it. It's not a lack of discipline. To me, the rest is very important."

How much sleep do you need? In order to get the right amount of much-needed sleep, endurance athletes listen to their bodies and let what feels natural and comfortable dictate their behavior. John Howard needs between six and nine hours of sleep. Lyn Brooks likes to get nine hours, sometimes ten.

You'll find that working out on a regular basis keeps the body in fine working order, so *all* normal functions—like sleeping—are enhanced. You might even find that the *quality* of your sleep improves.

The formula? Push your body until it tells you to stop and then sleep for as long as you can. Average sleeping time for most adults is between six and nine hours a night. Experiment to find how much is right for you by listening to your body and following its natural rhythm. Enjoy the wonderful weary feeling that comes from pushing yourself—and sleep.

9

Finding the Marathon in You

A friend came up to me on the street one day and said, "I was just down in Florida and I tried to swim in the ocean. A half mile seemed really far. How do you swim for so long? Can I increase my distance?"

"Yes," I told him.

Pushing back your physical limits is one of the best ways to get endurance into your life. Perhaps you are dreaming of the English Channel, the Ironman triathlon, or a bike trip across America. Or you may wish simply to begin an exercise program and stay healthy for life. Maybe you're already working out and are interested in safely challenging yourself further.

Here's how to begin an exercise program if you don't already have one and safely increase your workouts if you are already working out.

Six Steps to Finding
the Marathon in You

1. Choose a Sport You Enjoy

The more you enjoy the sport or activity, the better you'll do. Not everyone will find pleasure in the water or on the track. This is something you are choosing for yourself. No one is paying you or giving you extra incentive to do it. It must be something from which you find personal satisfaction, or you are simply not going to do it.

Experiment. Try running, biking, swimming, aerobics classes, tennis, softball, rowing, ice skating, cross-country skiing—anything. Get out of your business clothes, put on the right shoes, and *do* something.

There are clues indicating how much you enjoy your chosen activity. You will know you really like it, maybe even love it with passion, if you keep wanting to do more, if it makes you feel great when you're done, if it starts reflecting positively in your attitude, your skin, your work, and your personal life. You can always find the time for something you *really* want to do.

On the other hand, if you need to talk yourself into going to the gym, if changing into workout clothes is a good excuse not to bother, if you can never find the time, this is not the sport for you.

If you must wear a Walkman to get through a workout, chances are you find the activity too boring to keep you interested in and of itself. You want to find something that holds your attention and allows you to feel and enjoy what is happening inside your body while you exercise. When your body is absorbed, your mind is free to explore and create.

It's okay to occasionally use a Walkman or enjoy the company of a partner to vary your routine. But always relying on an outside influence is not a great idea. It's too handy an excuse not to bother when the Walkman is broken or your partner is sick. Ten to one, you'll skip your workout. Don't give yourself the excuse.

2. Take the First Step

You have found something you enjoy and want to begin. The first step is always the hardest. Give yourself a push— maybe some tangible reward—or talk a friend into starting with you. When you first stand at the side of the pool, it may look very big and very wet. Commit yourself, take a deep breath, and jump in. The water will always feel cold at first (even an 80° pool is almost twenty degrees colder than your body). Once you're submerged and moving, you won't feel so cold. And when you run, the first step on the pavement will always be a jolt, but as you continue to run, your feet and legs will adapt and the ground will not feel so hard. The other side is not as far away when you approach it stroke by stroke or step by step.

3. Start Slowly

The fastest way to hate exercising is to do *too much too fast*. The idea is to stay fit and healthy until you die. It took twenty, forty, maybe sixty years to get into the shape you are in now. You are not going to become an Adonis in two days. If you try to run ten miles your first time out, you are bound to rip or pull some ligament or muscle. People who begin exercise programs fast and hard quit early on because it hurts too much and they can't bear the thought of so much pain day after day. Who can blame them? Exercising doesn't have to be that painful.

Fitness takes time; be prepared. Thirty minutes a day for four or five days a week can be found in even the busiest of life-styles. Those thirty minutes a day will give back a lifetime of health.

If you've never worked out before and begin with thirty-minute sessions a few times a week, you will notice improvement almost immediately. The better shape you are in, the longer it will take to see improvement. Olympic athletes, for example, slave for months to knock a fraction of a second off their times.

If you work out already and want to go farther, begin by pacing slowly. Find a speed you think you could maintain indefinitely. As you go farther at that pace, you will find you can also go a little faster and still keep up your distance. You can't sprint at the beginning of an endurance workout and expect to last.

Start slowly and build. Slow starters last longer.

4. STICK WITH IT

Whether you choose to increase your distance or stay where you are, keep up with your exercise program. You are setting your fitness pace for life. Choose a specific time slot three or four days a week and put it on your calendar in ink. Stick with it. Consistency is the key.

5. TEST YOUR LIMITS

Let's say you are swimming a half mile or running three miles or biking ten miles quite comfortably right now. How far can you go? Take this test.

Set a goal to *double* your distance. Be sure to listen to your body, and consult your physician before you set this goal. Having done this, make an appointment with yourself to do it. Be sure it won't interfere with potential business commitments. For example, an actor should not schedule his "test" during prime audition hours because if he gets a call, guess which booking he's going to keep. If someone calls you to ask you to a movie or to a fancy dinner, enticing though the offer may be, say, "Sorry, no. I have a date to test my limits." This appointment is more important than dinner or a film. This is for you, for your health and well-being. You can't count on a film being worth your money, but you can bank on your workout being worth your time.

When the hour arrives, forget the excuses. Saying "I forgot to buy new running shoes," "I'd rather be sleeping," or "I'll do it tomorrow" is for wimps.

As you test your limits on double-your-distance day, expect to feel discomfort as your muscles burn and sweat pours. Your test may feel like the following scenario:

> I was putting in a hard four-mile run after several weeks of not running at all. When I started out, everything hurt. My knee bothered me, my ankles were stiff, my shoulders felt heavy. My fingers tingled as the blood rushed from my hands to the muscles in my legs. I kept running.

> By the middle of the second mile, the aches had faded. My face was flushed and I was damp all over. My body was warmed up. I smiled and picked up my pace. During the third mile, my legs reminded me that I had not run for a while. Even my butt ached as gravity pulled down on my body. I began to wonder if it was really necessary to run all four miles. I told myself the goal was four and I could reach it without hurting myself. I pulled out every trick in the book to fulfill my promise to myself—four miles.

> I began counting my strides. I concentrated on my form and promised myself a large bowl of chocolate chocolate-chip ice cream if I finished. When the last quarter mile was in sight, I let myself go. I relaxed, took deep, full breaths, lengthened my stride, increased my pace and flew. I felt great as I raised my arms in triumph.

Do it. The triumph is double your distance away.

6. You Did It!

You passed your test. By doubling your distance, by reserving a special time each week to devote to your health, you have discovered you *do* have the time and the ability. You can't make excuses anymore.

Warning: Endurance is addictive.

After you "do it" you could be hooked. Once you've comfortably doubled your distance, it will be hard for you to do less. It's like moving into a house with two and a half bathrooms—it's hard to return to a place with only one.

To ward off injury, vary the intensity of your workouts—do your increased mileage one day, but less the next.

Soon you'll be wondering how much farther you can go.

Workout Tips

What Does Pushing Yourself Feel Like?

When I first started to push back my limits, I learned what athletic discomfort was—a place just past comfortable but short of pain. I experienced a dull soreness in every muscle, a light-headedness, and an aura of well-being.

Pushing to the Point of Pain Is Not a Gain

The phrase "no pain, no gain" is repeated over and over to inspire athletes to push harder and to get fitness enthusiasts to feel "the burn." The phrase should be corrected. It should be "no discomfort, no gain." To push beyond discomfort is to beg for injury. Severe pain is a warning. The body knows when it is being stressed and will tell you so.

WARNING PAIN

The warnings to be alert to are sharp, burning, sustained pain, light-headedness or dizziness, deep chest pain, feeling you may slip into unconsciousness, the inability to take a full breath, the cessation of perspiration. All of these are symptoms of serious ailments (see chapter 11 to understand what is happening inside the body as these ailments occur). These signals cannot be confused with discomfort. Their message is clear: *stop*.

POSITIVE PAIN

Discomfort varies in degree and has its own special rewards. If you are just starting out on a fitness program, you may experience discomfort after ten or twenty minutes of moderate running. You might feel dull (not sharp) aches, a little stiffness, creaking in the knees, a heaviness in the legs and arms, a strange tingling in the hands and feet, and maybe even a minor headache. Chances are your panting and moaning could be reduced by tossing away cigarettes, eliminating refined foods, eating foods rich in nutrients, and sticking with an exercise program. In no time at all, your body will adapt to the discomfort. The strange tingling in the hands and feet will become recognizable as blood circulating, the stiffness and creaking will disappear as you get loosened and warmed up, the blood circulating efficiently through your body will make you feel slightly flushed all over, and you will breathe deeply and easily.

When you start to work out consistently, your level of conditioning improves and, with it, your tolerance for discomfort. If you've never run for a mile, the mere thought of a marathon will make your quadriceps throb. Actual participation in a 26.2-mile run would most certainly cause injury and is not wise to attempt. However, as your running ability and mileage increase over time, you may find that a marathon could be completed with relative ease.

RELAXATION

When increasing your distance in any sport, the first and most important skill to master is relaxation. Relaxing doesn't mean being lazy, resting, or using poor technique; it means performing a physical activity with constant, unstressed motion. While doing any activity over time, whatever limbs, muscles, or ligaments are tight or ungiving will eventually cramp, hurt, tear, or break. The body can relax through exercise and become free of tension. This helps unclutter the head and aids in alleviating stress in any situation.

Be comfortable. If your clothing doesn't fit properly, if it snags or pulls, if you're too cold or too warm, you're not going to get far. Take the time to prepare for a workout before you begin. Think of careful preparation as a way of pampering yourself.

PROPER FORM

Good form is essential to all sports. Poor technique slows you down and wears you down faster. As you perform any physical activity over long periods of time, you'll want to perfect your form because you won't have the energy for anything less efficient.

To increase your endurance in biking, swimming, running, or at the health club, take some tips from the experts:

Swimming Tips

Choose a comfortable, well-fitted bathing suit. A suit that is too tight causes chafing and cutting; one that is too loose rides up and creates drag.

Finding the right goggles may be your toughest chore. You want a pair that don't leak, but are not so tight that they give you a headache. Experiment. The brand I swear by may not work for your face structure.

Freestyle is the most commonly used stroke for long distance; it is the most efficient and least exhausting and gets you where you're going fastest.

Two common problems keep people from being able to swim freestyle longer: overkicking and poor breathing habits. Overkicking can be solved by remembering that less is more. Kicking too much forces blood to the muscles in your legs and starves the muscles that need it—namely, the arms. That is wasteful.

When you go for distance, kick only enough to keep your legs horizontal in the water, enough so that they are not dragging your body down. Keep the knees and ankles loose, not tight. Kick just enough to create a subtle boiling action in the water. Work with a kickboard to strengthen and even out your kick.

Breathing is a difficult skill to master and can be learned only with practice. While you're swimming, the top of your hairline should be at the water line. To breathe, tip the chin out of the water just enough to suck in air without swallowing water. While learning how little a head turn is necessary to breathe, you may wind up swallowing some water at first. It won't hurt you—you'll adjust.

Lifting the head too far out of the water throws off your entire stroke and is wasted motion. To conserve energy while you swim, let the natural motion of your body propel you. Roll from side to side with each pull of the arm, enough so that the pressure of the arm and shoulder work is shared by the back. The more distance you're able to do, the more you'll want to breathe on both sides, because your neck will get sore lifting and breathing in only one direction. Practice will make bilateral breathing feel less awkward.

Efficiency is the key. The more relaxed and easy the movement, the less resistance you create. In general, keep your shoulders relaxed, your elbows high, and your stroke long. You use less energy and go faster when your stroke is clean and efficient.

Biking Tips

With help from John Howard

Your bicycle has to fit you properly or it will deter you from enjoying a long-distance workout. To test frame size, straddle the top bar while standing on the ground. Your crotch should be at least one inch above the tube. Also check the length from saddle to handlebars by putting your elbow from the front of the saddle and extending it to the handlebar stem. If your fingertips extend halfway across the horizontal stem, your bike is the right length.

Lots of people ride on bicycles that seem much too big or small for them. Most often the problem is the height of the saddle. You can tell if the seat height is right if, while seated, your leg is not fully extended at any time. Your knee should be slightly bent, even when the pedal is down. For proper saddle position, check to see whether the center of the kneecap is parallel to the middle of the pedal.

Learn how to use the gears. Putting effort into every stroke tires you too quickly. Using a too-high gear can stress ankles and knees. Maintain a high cadence or spin. At first, your feet will seem to whirl away too easily, but gradually you'll get used to letting your legs go fast and see that, over distance, you're putting out less effort.

The most frequent complaint on long-distance rides is soreness in the shoulders, neck, seat, hands, and lower back. This is caused by being in the same position for hours. To help alleviate soreness, shift positions. Move the hands around, placing the weight differently each time to lessen numbness created by resting on the handlebars. To relieve soreness in the seat, shift your sitting position. Get off your saddle on the uphills—that's what hills are for. It gives your seat a rest and stresses different leg muscles. Wiggle and stretch your toes to relax your feet. Changing posture over distance will relieve your back. Let your arms dangle, one at a time. Stretch them and swing them around—that will help reduce shoulder soreness and numbness in the hands.

Running Tips

With help from Stu Mittleman

First, you need good, comfortable running shoes. If you're going to be running on hard surfaces, choose shoes with a lot of cushion for shock absorption. After the first few runs you'll know by the condition of your feet (blisters, soreness) if the shoe fits.

Expect the body to go through some changes. Change by its very nature is discomforting and possibly painful. As you increase your mileage, the hamstrings and calves may tighten. Your feet will ache from the pounding.

Light stretching before and after each run will ease stress and tightening. Massage may help. Soaking your feet and keeping them raised when you get home at night may also ease pain.

To go distance, conserve energy. There's no need to lift each leg sky-high on every step. The torso and upper body should be relaxed, arms loose with elbows held slightly away from the body. The arms should move in opposition to the legs, balancing the body's movement. The shoulders should not tilt back and forth as you run. Keep the head up and don't watch your feet. Try to run evenly. Any imbalance in your step, a slight turnout of one knee, stressing your right over your left, will all turn into problems as you increase your distance. And breathe as deeply as you can from the abdomen.

Remember Stu's basic training: Running is not just running. Increasing distance means taking on other responsibilities. Running is stretching, rest, recovery, diet, strength exercises, flexibility, and cardiovascular training. If you think of running in its expanded form, the likelihood of getting hurt as you increase your distance is greatly diminished.

Tips on Health Club Workouts

With help from Steven Lichtman

When increasing your health club workout—whether you are taking more aerobics classes a week or starting up a new weight training program—do it gradually and listen to your body for signs of fatigue or stress.

Purposely begin at a low level. Psychologically, this will help you to see gains in your body's strength, flexibility, and tone. You will want to see these gains *gradually* rather than jumping in, pushing too hard, then feeling exhausted. If you do too much too soon, you might see a quick gain and then nothing more. *How much you do is not as important as having the patience to stick with what you are doing and being consistent.* A high level of intensity is not necessary; time, consistency, patience, and sticking to your exercise program will result in benefits.

Try to have fun. At New York University's Exercise Prescription Program, which Steven Lichtman runs, the workouts are designed to be pleasant and enjoyable. "If it's not fun, you're not going to do it, and if you don't do it, you don't get the benefits," says Lichtman.

You won't fit into jeans a size smaller or feel that healthy glow unless you push it a little. So go ahead and sweat; get your heart rate up where it will do you some good. Feel soreness. Look forward to the lovely weariness that comes from a good workout. The more you do, the more you can do. As you push your limits back farther and farther, you'll begin to have an understanding of how the endurance athlete pursues the ultimate challenge.

Whether you're a fitness enthusiast wishing to improve your health and your body or an endurance athlete setting out to swim around the world, go ahead and endure some positive pain.

10

How the Ultras
Train to Finish

There are no rules for how much to work out, how to train, what to eat. No one told the ultra-athletes how to train. They had to come up with their own training regimens based on their experience—and by listening to their own bodies. The training regimens of the ultras constantly evolve as each athlete learns more and more about his or her body's physiological reaction to endurance. The following regimens show how some ultra-athletes have trained for certain running, triathlon, and swimming events. They are specific to the event named. It is important to remember that the ultras built *carefully* and *slowly* to these programs. An amateur should not use these programs as a blueprint.

Stu Mittleman

Event:	1985 New Astley Belt Six-Day Race (winner) (one of four six-day races completed in a year)
Training time:	3 months
Hours spent:	6–9 hours a day
Mileage per week:	Ran or walked a total of 200 miles
Supplementary activity:	Acupressure
Length of taper:	2 weeks (100 miles in the first; 50 in the second)
Sleep:	7–9 hours a night
Diet:	High fiber, high carbohydrate; one glass of wine a day; no refined sugars, no caffeine

---

John Howard

Event:	1982 Race Across AMerica
Training time:	7 months

Hours spent:	Started at 3½–4 hours a day; gradually increased to 9 hours a day in the final 6–8 weeks
Mileage:	Early months 250–300 miles per week; gradually increased to 800 miles per week for the last 6 weeks
Supplementary activity:	Light running and light swimming
Length of taper:	7 days
Sleep:	8–9 hours a night
Diet:	Complex carbohydrates (same diet as usual plus carbo loading, but not depleting)

Julie Ridge

Event:	1983 Manhattan Island Double
Training time:	5 months
Hours spent:	4–5 hours, 5 or 6 days a week
Mileage per week:	Swam 20 miles for first 2 months; swam 30–35 miles for final 3 months
Supplementary activity:	Full Nautilus, light running, softball (for pleasure)

Length of taper:	10 days of gradual taper
Sleep:	6–8 hours per night
Diet:	Whole-grain carbohydrates, vegetables, all-natural ice cream (to keep weight on); little or no refined sugar, alcohol, caffeine, chemicals, or additives

Determining Mileage

How do the ultras determine the number of miles they put into their workouts?

When I began training for the English Channel swim and the Ironman triathlon, I heard all sorts of gauges for determining the mileage required per week. For triathlons I kept hearing that I should train two to three times the total distance of the race. For instance, when training for an Ironman, I was advised to do approximately 8 miles of swimming, over 300 miles of biking, and 50 to 60 miles of running per week.

That seemed logical for a 10- or 20-mile swim, a marathon run, or most triathlons. However, it lost its credibility as I began to wonder: Does that mean that Stu Mittleman has to run 1,000 miles a week to prepare for a 500-mile six-day run, or that Cindy Nicholas must put in over 100 miles of swimming per week for a double or triple crossing of the English Channel (a swim of between 41 and 61.5 miles)? Of course not. Such mileage is impractical and nearly impossible, in addition to being downright unhealthful. Therefore, a maximum must be determined, which may have little to do with the actual distance of the event.

For any swim over 20 miles, my maximum is anywhere between 30 and 35 miles a week. Paul Asmuth puts in double that with an average of 20,000 meters (approximately 13.5 miles) a day six days a week for six to twelve weeks to cover his entire racing season. That season includes four or five races from 18 to 28 miles, or an approximate total of 120 miles of swim racing in a period of five weeks. In 1982 Mittleman worked with one coach and put in between 80 and 120 miles of running per week for all his races. Howard's current maximum is about 300 miles a week whether it's for an Ironman or to set a new land speed record. Whether it's a shorter race for speed or a longer event, their maximum weekly mileage is about the same. It's how they divide the miles during the training session that varies—doing long- slow-distance, or interval training. (See chapter 11 for more on interval training.) Ultimately, once the body is in good shape and a maintenance level has been achieved, the endurance athlete is capable of handling any distance.

How to Prevent Overtraining

How do you know when your training is enough, too much, or too little? The most common problem among endurance athletes is overdoing it. Dedicated and disciplined, the athlete may ignore the body's signals telling him to slow down (see chapter 4). The beginner—the athlete who is just starting to increase his mileage—might not know when to back off or to slow down. He might mistake his staleness or lack of motivation—symptoms of overtraining—for laziness and keep going. The seasoned athlete knows that laziness is not one of his traits and recognizes the following symptoms as overtraining:

- An increase in morning pulse rate. An increase of four beats per minute over your normal resting pulse rate is a sign to slow down. (See the next chapter for how to take your pulse.)
- A dramatic increase in thirst. This indicates that your metabolism hasn't had the chance to slow down between workouts. It is demanding more water to stay in high gear.
- Edginess. Working out is a form of stress. Too much of it can make you as irritable as you get while standing in an endless line at the post office or getting your long-distance phone bill.
- Slower times on the track or in the water
- Having trouble falling asleep
- A radical change in appetite
- Feeling a lack of motivation

The remedy? Cool it. Eat better, sleep more, and reevaluate your overall training program. Take a day or two off—completely. Take in a double feature, see old friends, spend some time with the kids, read a good old-fashioned murder mystery. Whatever you do, enjoy yourself, take your mind off training, and *rest*.

Finding the Middle Road: Less Is More

Happily, we are discovering that *less is more*. After a number of months or years, once the mileage base is established, a high level of conditioning can be maintained with far fewer hours of work than were required to get there. The millionaire can practically live off his interest if he invests wisely and doesn't dip into his capital. You can, too, if your original training is rich enough.

In his fifth season on the professional marathon swimming circuit, Paul Asmuth developed a bicep tendon injury and could not work out for a while. His usual training of 20,000 meters a day for six weeks was shortened to one week. Still, he managed to complete all five races on the circuit, winning three of them and retaining his number-one ranking for the fifth straight year. Obviously, his solid capital, basic talent, and strong drive made up where his mileage was low.

John Howard trained eight to ten hours a day to win the 1981 Ironman triathlon. He committed himself to his training to such an extent that he had his phone disconnected so that he would not be bothered by the outside world. He trained hard and won the race.

In retrospect, he says he didn't enjoy that period at all. Howard felt that twenty years of hard training—from the Olympics to ultra-distance—had aged him. He now believes that he can achieve better results and be happier in the process by doing fewer hours of more highly concentrated work.

Stu Mittleman, too, wonders whether he'd be better off doing less mileage. "I am starting to question the wisdom of training eight to nine hours a day," he says. "I don't know if I'm getting any faster as a runner or if I'm going to run any farther because of the training. I might be past the point where it's doing any good. It is very hard to get into the mind-set that backing off is considered a step forward. That's a lesson I've accepted."

Be Prepared:
Don't Undertrain

In my limited training for the 1984 Ironman triathlon, I was worried that I had finally cut myself too short, that I would arrive in Hawaii without any interest to draw on. I discovered to my relief and surprise that I could finish with ease and pleasure. My minimal ten to thirteen workout hours per week, along with my background in endurance, were enough to reach my goal of finishing within the seventeen-hour cutoff.

I was lucky. Instead of discovering the minimum amount of training I could get away with, I could just as easily have learned what undertraining meant.

Undertraining is the flip side of overtraining. It is usually the result of inexperience and of overestimating one's abilities. Without the proper foundation the athlete risks drawing on interest he has not yet earned and dangerously depleting his capital. This can cause unnecessary pain and injury.

The only way to find your minimum daily training requirement is to experiment. Training eight to ten hours a day is practical and desirable for some of the competitive, elite athletes. Four to five hours a day is ample to meet the goals of others. You might find that a half hour to an hour a day (you might even be able to fit in up to two hours on some days) is enough to maintain an excellent level of fitness established over the years.

Recovery

No matter how long or short your workout is, your body begins to recover as soon as you stop exercising. Recovery can last for a few minutes or a few hours. Twenty-four to forty-eight hours after an Ironman triathlon or a marathon, an athlete who has resumed normal eating and resting will have restored his muscle glycogen.

Recovery for torn muscles or damaged joints or ligaments requires healing which can take at least a few weeks.

An ultra-endurance runner's recovery time is usually longer than that of a long-distance swimmer or cyclist. Running is tougher on the body because you are generating a strong force against your bones and ligaments with the impact of each step. This stresses the knees and can cause the muscles, ligaments, and cartilage already under tension to tear. Your body has less impact to resist on a bicycle and none to resist in the water.

For endurance athletes one indication of recovery time is how soon after completing an event they can do it again. On the pro swimming circuit Paul Asmuth repeats a nine-to-ten-hour swim every Sunday for five weeks. Stu Mittleman has joked that he never recovers from a six-day run.

Strength training is a good example of the workout/ recovery pattern. People who lift weights are advised to alternate the days of their workout, never doing it two days in a row. The muscles need to recover because they are stretched and weakened. On a microscopic level they are broken down. A day away from weights gives the muscles time to recover by repairing injured tissue—and to grow stronger.

Although recovery time depends on the length and rigorousness of the workout, it also depends on your physical condition at the outset. The more time you've put into training and the better shape you're in, the *less* time it will take you to recover. Some studies of runners show that the people who get injured most often are those who run inconsistently. For example, if you run between thirty and forty miles a week, you are less likely to get injured than if you run twenty miles one week, don't run the next, and then do twenty miles the following week. Your body *adapts* to the mileage and stress you're putting it through and doesn't injure as easily.

To get an idea of what recovery time is on a smaller scale, you can do a simple test that is conducted at many health clubs. It's called the pulse recovery test, and the point of it is to see how fast your heart rate returns to a resting rate after being pushed and beating faster.

When you first come into the gym, take your pulse to find out your resting rate so you'll have a means for comparison. Begin by slowly jogging or cycling on a stationary bike for one to three minutes to get your body warmed up. Then for two minutes and fifteen seconds, push as hard as you can. Take your pulse during those last fifteen seconds, while you're exercising, to determine whether you have reached your target heart rate (you should not exceed it). (*See* How to Determine Your Target Heart Rate, below.) Stop exercising altogether, wait for one minute, and then take your pulse. Wait another minute, than take it again. Wait and take it a third time. You will have four numbers plus the resting pulse rate you started with. Compare them. Is the last pulse you took close to your resting rate? In some people it is. Notice how long it took your body to resume—or to get close to—its normal heart rate. A quick recovery time means your cardiovascular system is well trained and is working superbly.

How to Determine
Your Target Heart Rate (THR)

Your target heart rate (THR) is the rate at which you should work to increase both lung and heart capacity, and to improve the heart's ability to circulate blood.

To calculate your THR, take your pulse (see the next chapter for instructions) in the morning *before* you get out of bed. This is your resting heart rate (RHR). Then follow this formula:

1. Subtract your age from 220 (for men) or 226 (for women).
2. Subtract your RHR from the result.
3. Multiply this result by .70.
4. Add your RHR to this result for your THR.

For example, a forty-year-old man with an RHR of 68 would calculate:

```
220 − 40 (his age)   = 180
180 − 68 (his RHR) = 112
112 × .70            =   78.40
78.40 + 68 (RHR)   = 146.40, his target heart rate
```

11

Journey Through the Body

Why does exercise make us feel healthy? What exactly is going on inside us, underneath what we can see? Where does our energy come from? And how do we use it? We're about to take you on a journey through a strong, healthy body as it goes through the paces of a workout.

Where Does Movement Begin?

Any physical activity starts in the brain. When you get the idea to move or to exercise, the brain begins sending electrical messages via nerve tissue to the spinal cord, which, in turn, relays them to the muscles. A two-way communication begins as the muscles report back to the brain on conditions such as pain or temperature. The communication between these electrical currents goes back and forth, with the spinal cord acting as the impulse transmitter.

When you decide to exercise, one of the first areas in the body to receive an electrical nerve impulse is the adrenal glands, which are located above the kidneys. They start to put out a hormone known as adrenaline, or epinephrine, which is secreted in response to excitement or stress.

You might feel the effects of the stress hormone: Your heart rate will accelerate, your blood pressure will go up, and your muscle tone will increase. "It may feel like you're nervous or anxious, but it's a real functional adaptation; it's the way your body starts to get ready for what's to come," explains Dr. Doug Hiller, who conducted a study on endurance exercise at the Institute for Environmental Medicine at the University of Pennsylvania and at the Campbell Clinic at the University of Tennessee's College of Health Science, focusing on the effects of prolonged, intense exercise on athletes.

Where Does Energy Come From?

Food is the main source of all our fuel. The body uses two major sources of food as energy: fats and carbohydrates. The primary job of protein is to repair and build muscle tissue.

As a source of energy, carbohydrate is the most efficient. Unlike fat, it is easily broken down into simple sugars and can be quickly used by the body. It is also the main fuel supply for the central nervous system. The liver absorbs the simple sugars from the blood and converts them to glucose.

Glucose is the body's immediate fuel. The first one hundred grams of glucose are stored in the liver. The rest goes into the muscles. When glucose is stored in the liver and muscles, it is called glycogen. If you've eaten more carbohydrate than you need, the excess sugars are converted and stored as fat in what is known as adipose tissue.

The limiting factor of each source? You can't store much liver glycogen at a time, so you don't have much of it to use. It is also limited because it is needed to fuel tissues other than muscles. Fatty acids, on the other hand, are plentiful, but are more difficult to transport. They are not soluble in blood, so they must be transported in a soluble protein called albumin, which exists only in small amounts.

GOING FARTHER BELOW THE SURFACE: ENERGY MOLECULES

Although our energy comes from food, the protein, carbohydrates, and fats you eat are not directly used as fuel. First, they are broken down into food molecules. Trapped inside these molecules is chemical energy—the basis of our fuel supply. To get the chemical energy out of the molecules, other molecules called enzymes serve as a catalyst for chemical activity. Energy is created within the body as chemical bonds split and come together. This activity takes place on the cellular level in the molecules within each cell called the mitochondria.

THE SOURCE OF ALL ENERGY IN THE BODY: ATP

Once the food you've eaten has been broken down into molecules, we really get down to the source of all energy— the activity going on within the cells.

The end product of digestion is a chemical compound called ATP, or adenosine triphosphate. ATP is known as

138

"the energy currency" because it is the basis for *all* forms of biological activity. It not only carries energy but also supplies energy for all biological work, including digestion, nerve transmission, circulation, muscle contraction, gland secretion, and building new tissue.

REGENERATING ATP

There is only a small amount of ATP stored in each cell. In fact, throughout the body at any one time there is only enough energy to fuel it for several seconds, which is why we need to process ATP constantly for continuous energy. *Our whole energy-producing system exists for the sole purpose of regenerating ATP.*

There are three ways or pathways through which the body makes energy or ATP: the CP pathway, the lactate acid pathway, and the aerobic energy pathway.

The CP Pathway

Some of the energy for ATP is supplied by a high-energy compound called creatine phosphate (CP). This compound is known as "the energy reservoir" because its energy concentration is about three to five times greater than that of ATP. Because of its high concentration, when CP is split, its phosphate molecule links directly to a molecule called ADP (adenosine diphosphate). When linked to this phosphate, ADP becomes ATP, thus completing the energy cycle. Then ATP is broken into ADP and CP and they, in turn, are reconverted back to ATP. The energy cycle is repeated over and over again because the body is in constant need of energy and continues to break down ATP to fulfill that need.

This ATP-CP activity is a quick-energy system, used in extremely high intensity work such as a dash or sprint. This quick-energy system is an anaerobic pathway, meaning that the body doesn't use oxygen as part of the chemical process of creating energy. It comes into play when your activity is so strenuous that your body is not taking in sufficient oxygen to produce ATP at the time when you need it. According to Steven Lichtman, director of the exercise physiology program at New York University's Recreation Department, this type of energy only lasts for about eight seconds and is called free energy because it doesn't have to be synthesized. "That doesn't mean that you will stop working at the end of those eight seconds," explains Lichtman. "However, you won't be able to work at 100 percent of your speed."

The Lactate Acid Pathway

Once the first energy pathway has been depleted, you use a second anaerobic system called the lactate acid system. Like the first, it produces energy quickly and you use it quickly. It also produces a by-product called lactic acid, which is believed to cause muscle fatigue and pain. (For more on lactic acid, see "The Difference Between Anaerobic and Aerobic Energy" below.)

The Aerobic Energy Pathway

The third system is an aerobic energy pathway. "Aerobic work is long, low-level work. It is how we spend our daily lives: walking, doing desk work," says Lichtman. "Aerobic energy is used for slow, long-term expenditure because it is a slow-producing system. It produces a lot of energy, slowly and cleanly." The only factor that limits the use of aerobic energy is the amount of fuel or glycogen available to the muscles. (For more on glycogen supply, see "What Causes Fatigue?" later in this chapter.) In most cases, your body can store enough energy to get you from morning to evening or from meal to meal.

The Difference Between Anaerobic and Aerobic Energy

> *Anaerobic = short-term, high-intensity*
> *Aerobic = long-term, low-intensity*

Throughout the course of a day we use both anaerobic and aerobic energy systems. When we run for a bus or lift a heavy bag of groceries, we use anaerobic energy. We also use short, intense bursts of energy for some movements in sports. Games of basketball and tennis, for example, combine both anaerobic and aerobic energy, since they require both short, intense bursts of energy and sustained movements like running up and down the court.

Anaerobic energy is used when lifting weights. It is also used for speed work and for interval training, which we'll explore shortly.

Activities requiring aerobic energy, on the other hand, have been shown to be beneficial to our health, since they improve the cardiovascular system and help us to battle cardiovascular disease. (Anaerobic activities do neither because they do not accelerate the heart rate for long enough periods of time.)

The other important difference between anaerobic and aerobic work is that when you are working anaerobically, you are building up lactic acid, and when you are working aerobically, you are not. (If we were to use anaerobic energy for everyday activities, we would be building up lactic acid and feeling fatigue in our muscles.)

HOW THE ENERGY-PRODUCING SYSTEM WORKS WHILE YOU EXERCISE

You are in a *steady state* when you are doing aerobic exercise over a period of time. Your body is producing energy and it might be producing some lactic acid, but not enough to feel any discomfort. "When you do aerobic work, lactic acid levels rise gently, level off, or decline as you go," says Lichtman. "Often, you are reutilizing the lactic acid as energy, and levels are so low that you don't feel it."

We use the aerobic energy system—and are in a steady state—during most activities in daily life, although this use of the aerobic system is different from *training* ourselves aerobically because the *rate* at which we are working is much higher when we exercise.

Working at a desk is a steady-state activity. Walking is a steady state, jogging is a steady state. Sprinting is not. In endurance events you are in a steady state until you run out of glycogen stores and you "hit the wall" or your body is no longer getting rid of the lactic acid as fast as you are producing it. You are no longer in a steady state when you begin to build up lactic acid.

When you continue on after reaching the steady state, you are getting close to what is known as the *anaerobic threshold*. "The threshold is the point where your body can no longer sustain the work through the aerobic energy system," explains Lichtman. "So the anaerobic system has to produce a lot of energy and the lactic acid level begins rising as opposed to rising gently and leveling off as it does in aerobic exercise. When you reach the threshold, the acid rises dramatically and you start to feel the effects of it."

You can push back your anaerobic threshold with *interval training,* which is usually used by competitive athletes who want to improve their speed or endurance. (Warning: Because interval training raises the heart rate, it might be a risk to people who smoke, are overweight, have high blood pressure, or have a history of cardiovascular disease in their family. Especially if you are thirty-five years old or older, you should consult a doctor before beginning any aerobic program.)

Here's how interval training works: Run, swim, or bike a short distance at 95 to 100 percent effort. Feel the lactic acid burn. Rest after each set enough to catch your breath. (Some athletes make the rest period just as long as the time it took to do the work.) If you are averaging a seven-minute running mile and you go faster than that, you'll feel your anaerobic threshold. In time you won't feel that threshold until you're pushing a 6.45-minute mile.

You can use interval training—as opposed to long, slow, steady training—to increase your speed and to push back your anaerobic threshold. It will help your body build a resistance to the feeling of lactic acid and to its effects on your muscles and overall endurance.

WHAT'S HAPPENING IN THE MUSCLES DURING EXERCISE?

ATP is the energy source for muscle contraction. Within each muscle fiber are rodlike structures called myofibrils. Inside these are thin and thick protein filaments. Muscle contraction occurs when these thin and thick filaments pull or slide over one another.

All of us have two kinds of muscle fibers—fast twitch and slow twitch—interspersed throughout the body. The fast-twitch fibers have a higher activity level of the enzyme that activates ATP, making their speed of contraction twice as fast as that of slow-twitch fibers. Fast-twitch fibers perform well in short bursts of energy, while the slow perform best in aerobic endurance activities.

Most sports physiologists agree that your percentage of each fiber type is genetically predetermined. In some cases a muscle biopsy can determine what kind of fiber you have in a particular limb. "Physiologists measure muscle by stimulating it to measure how fast it contracts," says Dr. Hiller. "The slow twitch doesn't contract as rapidly."

But some physiologists claim that muscle biopsy is questionable as an overall measure of muscle type because different muscles in the body can be fast twitch or slow twitch. In a runner there will be more fast-twitch fibers in the legs and more slow-twitch in the arms if they are underused.

Exercise physiologists also claim that you can't change the *amount* of fiber type you have, but that you can train fiber types to take on the characteristics of the other. New research has found that there are different types of fast-twitch fibers called type IIA, IIB, and IIC. Type IIA has great potential to become slow twitch or to perform aerobically. Type IIC may be able to switch between both fast and slow twitch. Type IIB has great anaerobic potential and may not be able to become slow twitch.

What Does Body Fat Do for Us?

We need a certain amount of body fat to survive. Our bodies are composed of lean tissue (muscle) and fat. Within our bodies there are two kinds of fat: essential fat, which surrounds and protects nerves and organs such as the heart, liver, kidney, brain, and female reproductive organ; and subcutaneous, or storage, fat, directly under the skin, which insulates the body. In women accumulation of a certain amount of fat—especially in the breasts, hips, and thighs—is promoted by the hormone estrogen. Too much weight loss or body fat loss could result in amenorrhea, a condition in which a woman stops menstruating altogether. Doctors aren't exactly sure what causes menstrual irregularity or amenorrhea, since not all female athletes with low body fat percentages are affected.

When we weigh ourselves on the gym scale, we measure our overall weight, which is a combination of muscle and fat. However, it's helpful to distinguish between fat weight and muscle weight. How much of your body's composition is fat and how much is muscle?

Muscle is denser—and weighs more—than fat. If you gain weight while on an exercise program (specifically one involving aerobics and weight training, which build muscle tissue), the weight you put on could be muscle, not fat. If you continue with your exercise program, your percentage of body fat will gradually drop.

There are several ways to measure body composition. Hydrostatic or underwater weighing is the most accurate method, but also the most difficult for many individuals (you are placed in a tank of water and must expel all air from the lungs while underwater). Lichtman recommends this method for scientific research and for ultra-athletes concerned about a 1 percent change in their body fat level. He suggests all others use the skin-fold method (accurate to within 3 percent of hydrostatic weighing), in which a skilled tester uses a pair of calipers, an instrument especially designed to measure skin thickness.

Body Fat Percentages

	Women	Men
Necessity	12%	3%
Ideal for active 25-year-old	18–22%	15–20%
Olympic-caliber or endurance runners and cyclists	12–15%	3–5%

Endurance runners and cyclists want to carry as little body fat as possible, since it is an insulator and they need to eliminate as much heat as possible. Conversely, long-distance swimming is different from most other sports in that body fat comes in handy to keep the swimmer buoyant and to insulate against the cold. Because skilled female endurance athletes have 9 to 10 percent more body fat than men of the same caliber, females often have an advantage over male swimmers. According to Lichtman, one study predicted that women are projected to pass men in distance swimming. "Swimming is one sport where top women swimmers will be competing with top men," says Lichtman. "Men's strength will help them, but women's fat will help *them* because they won't have to expend as much energy." In fact, women have been successfully competing against men for decades. World records for the fastest one-way crossing of the Catalina Channel and one-way and two-way crossings of the English Channel are all held by women.

What Causes Fatigue?

No one knows completely why we get tired and need to rest or sleep. It's a question biophysicists and physiologists are still working on. "Fatigue is not a well-understood phenomenon," explains Lichtman. "No one is sure why you get tired. Is it because you build up lactic acid? Is it because you run out of energy? Is it from the transmitter inside the fibers?"

Physiologists speculate that one of the causes of fatigue is that the neuromuscular junctions—where the nerve impulses are transmitted—get tired, similar to the way any muscle tires while doing very high speed frequent contractions.

One of the better known reasons for fatigue is simply running out of fuel. The fuel you're using to exercise with today comes from the foods you ate last night and this morning. When your muscles run out of muscle glycogen and you experience "hitting the wall," the muscles have run out of gas and you feel exhausted. If you don't replenish your fuel by eating or drinking, your body will attempt to use fat as fuel. But fat does not burn efficiently without the presence of carbohydrate in the system. So your body will compensate for what it lacks by trying to make more carbohydrate. "Inside the body, you're going to start breaking down the protein that's there, to rebuild the glucose molecule, so you'll have carbohydrate to burn," explains Dan Sikowitz, an exercise physiologist who directs the fitness evaluation program at New York City's Biofitness Institute. "You'll be able to continue on, but you'll be exhausted."

For a trained marathon runner twenty miles seems to be the point where most hit the wall. "An untrained person will run out of muscle glycogen long before a marathoner," says Lichtman. "They will hit their own wall."

Replacing food and fluid during an event helps an athlete avoid the fatigue caused by hitting the wall. That's why athletes replenish their energy supply by drinking and eating periodically during long endurance events. Drinking water replaces the water you lose through sweating. Eating during an event provides glucose to the working muscles and to the central nervous system and helps to prevent dizziness or light-headedness.

A *drop* in body temperature can cause sleepiness, which occurs as hypothermia sets in, for example. As the body cools down, the heart slows and you fall asleep. Some forms of anesthesia work by cooling down the body to make the individual sleepy.

Lactic acid buildup is another possible reason for fatigue. The pain of lactic acid buildup is actually caused by the acid's action on the muscles. Your pH is usually normal, but because lactate is an acid, its presence throws off the pH balance in the body and slows down the chemical processes inside the body.

When athletes have lactic acid buildup, they try to tolerate the pain. According to some speculation, athletes are able to push past the pain because of chemical compounds, called endorphins, that are released from the brain. Their effect on the body has been compared to that of the pain-killing drug morphine, but the medical community isn't sure exactly why or how endorphins affect the body. Some physiologists claim that when muscles are fatigued, endorphins cut off the sensory impulses that transmit the message of pain, so the athlete doesn't *feel* the hurt. Other theories say that the endorphins actually break down the lactic acid. Whatever it is that happens physiologically, the athlete feels a druglike high, a euphoria, a feeling beyond the pain.

Muscle soreness is another cause of fatigue. This type of fatigue often comes the day after a workout and usually occurs when you exercise muscles that are not fully adapted to the stress you are placing upon them.

The Effects of Exercise
on the Body

Physical exercise results in benefits to your health, both short- and long-term. Some of the benefits are immediate: You might feel less tired and have renewed energy and a healthy glow to your skin. Lifelong effects include a healthy, strong body and heightened energy levels.

WHY SWEAT?

Take the concept of "warming up" literally. When you warm up before exercising, your body temperature will start to rise. Your muscles are more efficient at about 99° or 100° than they are at 98.6°.

You'll start to feel warm all over and maybe a little flushed. "One of the effects of the temperature rising is that it causes you to have more surface blood flow," says Dr. Hiller. "It's a cycle. When you exercise, your muscles begin to produce heat. In order to get rid of that heat, the blood vessels at your skin dilate, which causes you to flush and lose some of that heat."

Sweating is the outward sign of the changes going on inside your body. When you break out in a sweat, your body's core temperature is rising.

There are about 3 million sweat glands spread over the surface of your body. When you sweat in response to a change in temperature or exercise, you activate the eccrine glands, which secrete a weak saline solution. But you have other glands as well. These are the apocrine glands, and they are located only in certain parts of the body—the groin, underarms, nipples, and buttocks. Anger, sexual arousal, and nervousness activate these glands. You can tell which kind of sweat you are emitting by the way it smells. Eccrine sweat smells good and clean. The secretion of apocrine glands mixes with bacteria to cause a pungent acrid odor.

Eccrine sweat serves more than one purpose; it is your body's built-in cooling and cleaning system and works the same way as saunas and steam baths do. When you sweat, water appears on the surface of the skin so it can evaporate and carry off excess heat, making the skin feel cooled.

It's important to remember that it is evaporation that makes sweating effective in cooling you; just having water on your skin won't do anything for you. Sweat that just rolls off your body or pools in one spot doesn't cool you down. Clothes that don't let your skin breathe may make you sweat, but they can be dangerous because they don't permit evaporation. Sauna suits are one example. They will make your body temperature go up and cause you to sweat. But because you are covered by the suit, your sweat won't be able to evaporate. The body's natural cooling system won't be able to work, and heat illness—dehydration or stroke—could occur.

THE EFFECT OF EXERCISE ON THE BONES

Physiologically, your whole body is changing when you exercise. According to Dr. Hiller, even your bones become stronger. The more you stress a bone, the more it is able to resist that stress and hence avoid breaking. Explains Dr. Hiller, "Most people think of bone as being like rock. It's not. It's as alive as any other part of the body."

When you exercise, you strengthen the ligaments and tendons which attach the bones to each other and attach the muscles to the bone. In addition, the cartilage inside the joints becomes thicker. By strengthening the ligaments and tendons, you ward off injury to the joints, which are held in place by the ligaments and tendons.

Research shows that weight-bearing exercise also helps to keep your bones strong as you grow older and, coupled with regular intake of the nutrient calcium, can help to prevent the onset of osteoporosis, a condition in which bones become thin and porous. Both help to increase bone density. A University of North Carolina study found that women between the ages of fifty-five and seventy-five who were athletic had bone density which was 15 to 20 percent greater than women their age who were sedentary.

When older people have not kept in shape over the

years, their bones may be brittle. They should consult a physician or health club trainer before beginning a fitness program. And when they do work out, they should start out with a gentle exercise program that will not stress their bones too much.

The bones of children and preadolescents are still growing and forming. Intense exercise—like running distance or weight training—is not usually recommended until after puberty. The activity might not be specifically harmful for the bones, but they won't benefit from the exercise as do the bones of adults.

THE EFFECTS OF EXERCISE ON THE RESPIRATORY SYSTEM

As you begin to work out, you'll notice that you begin to breathe more deeply. During the first few minutes of activity, your oxygen intake rises rapidly because your body's demand is immediately greater than it was when you were standing still. Your muscles need oxygen to generate ATP, to reuse waste products such as lactic acid for energy, and to exhale other wastes such as carbon dioxide and water.

Air enters through the nose and mouth. By the time it reaches the lungs, it has been filtered, humidified, and adjusted to body temperature. The lungs themselves are not a muscle, but must rely on the muscles around them—the rib cage, diaphragm, and abdominals—to expand and contract while inhaling and exhaling.

The difference between a sedentary person's lungs and an athlete's lungs is not size (lungs do not get bigger with exercise), but how efficiently they work and how strong the surrounding muscles are to support the lungs. Use the image of the lung as a balloon. The more you exercise, and therefore the harder you breathe, the more you'll blow up your balloon and the stronger the muscles surrounding it will be. According to Dr. Hiller, there is no difference in the development of a runner's, biker's, or swimmer's lungs. The lungs of any athlete working close to their aerobic maximum will develop the same way. *A body that is exercised regularly can take in double the amount of air as one that is not exercised regularly,* which means you will be able to process more energy (ATP) and do so without fatigue for a longer period of time.

To see how hard your lungs can work, physiologists test what's known as an athlete's VO2 Max—the maximum amount of oxygen that an athlete can consume. There are several ways to do the test, depending on the physical condition of the athlete. Sedentary people are tested by walking on the treadmill. For his study on endurance, Dr. Hiller tested trained athletes by connecting them to an electrical cardiogram and a mouthpiece which collects their expired gases. They began by walking on the treadmill, then they did a 10-minute-mile jog followed by an 8.5-minute-mile jog. Then the top of the treadmill was elevated (to simulate a difficult uphill run) by an increase of 2.5 percent every three minutes. As the treadmill elevates, the athlete uses more and more oxygen until he hits a point which is difficult to maintain. He is almost at his physical limit. Depending on the individual, the test lasts between fifteen and twenty minutes. The athlete's oxygen consumption is measured by how much he is expiring.

As an athlete's body is conditioned into a leaner, meaner working machine, VO2 Max increases. But there is a limit to how high that Max will go. Each person's VO2 Max is predetermined by genetic composition—you can't consume more oxygen than your VO2 Max.

How does oxygen get to the working muscles that need it? Oxygen travels around the body in the red blood cells. It enters the bloodstream in the lungs, where blood-carrying capillaries and alveoli, small membranous sacs filled with air, exist right next to one another. The oxygen passes through the membrane of the alveoli into the inside of the capillary and attaches itself to the hemoglobin in the red blood cell. The blood is then pumped through the lungs and to the rest of the body. For the average person, during each moment at rest, about 250 milliliters of oxygen leave the alveoli and enter the blood. For a trained endurance athlete doing heavy exercise, twenty-five times that amount is transferred through the alveoli.

THE EFFECT OF EXERCISE ON THE CARDIAC SYSTEM

The cardiovascular and respiratory systems work together intimately, but the system that changes most dramatically inside the body as you begin to exercise is the cardiac system. "Your cardiac output—the amount of blood that is pumped per minute—can increase eighteen to twenty times," explains Dr. Hiller. "When you aren't exercising, a lot of blood is in your liver, digesting food, and it is as if you aren't pumping very much. It is almost as if some of the blood supply to your muscles is shut down. When you start to exercise, all the blood vessels going to and from your muscles dilate so that more blood goes through them and goes through them faster. The size of the blood vessels increases so that the blood can go through them, and more channels open up in the muscle so that the muscle itself actually gets bigger. That's what weight lifters call pumping up."

Blood pressure is a measure of how hard your heart and your blood vessels are working. When you've had blood pressure tests in the past, your doctor or fitness trainer rolled up your sleeve and wrapped a cuff around your biceps. You were probably told that normal readings are about 120/80, the average for healthy people, which is used as a level of comparison.

What does this mean? Picture it this way: The numbers show how high your heart can push a column of mercury. The top number stands for the systolic pressure, a measure of the maximum amount of blood the heart delivers as it ejects blood into the artery. The lower number is the diastolic, or resting, pressure, when no blood is being pumped into the system and the area is at rest. When you exercise, your systolic pressure goes up. In weight lifters it may go up to 350 or 400 at the instant that they're lifting. During a race, an endurance athlete's systolic pressure might go up to between 180 and 250. Immediately after you exercise, the top number comes down. The bottom number, your resting pressure, may go up slightly while you exercise and will come down when you stop. In normal, healthy individuals the resting pressure stays the same even while they exercise.

The more you exercise, the lower your resting blood pressure will be. It is as though your blood vessels are also getting in shape. They are developing neurovascular tone, which means they are becoming elastic or flexible. They don't resist when called upon to expand and contract. The more elastic and flexible your blood vessels are, the easier it is for the blood to flow back to the heart and the lower your diastolic pressure will be. The harder it is for the blood to flow and the more resistance there is in the vessels, the higher the number.

Blood pressure is like water pressure in a hose. If you turn it up high, the pressure will be higher as more water pumps through it; thus, more stress will be placed on the walls of the hose. If you capped the end of the hose and turned it on high, the hose would bulge and possibly burst. That's what's happening to your blood vessels when you have high blood pressure. Very high blood pressure is dangerous because the pressure can rupture small blood vessels. When this occurs in your brain, it's called a stroke.

The heart is a muscle. When you exercise, you strengthen it the same way you strengthen your legs or your arms. If you exercise regularly, your heart rate goes up as it pumps more blood—maybe five times as much—with each stroke. If you don't exercise often, your heart will beat about four times as fast as it did at rest, but it *won't* pump more blood.

To bring about a change in your cardiovascular condition, current research indicates that you should do continuous aerobic exercise for a minimum of twenty minutes to a half hour three times a week. The heart will change in two ways: It will get larger, and it will pump more slowly. "The enlargement and the slowing down of the heart is a reaction to stressing it," explains Dr. Hiller. But you have to exercise *enough* to stress your heart, and you have to stress it in a positive way. This is done by aerobic exercise, making your heart work for twenty or thirty minutes at a time. According to Dr. Hiller, these workouts should affect your heart in about three to six weeks.

How to Take Your Pulse

The best way to find out how slowly your heart beats is to take your pulse first thing in the morning before you get up, since that is a true test of your body when it is at rest. The best places to take your pulse are on the throat and wrist. Always use your three middle fingers. Never use your thumb; it has a strong pulse of its own and can throw off your count. Find your Adam's apple in the center front of your neck. Hold your hand in a horizontal position and push your three fingers gently to the side of the Adam's apple between your windpipe and your neck muscle. Feel the pulse beat. To get your resting pulse rate, hold the fingers there and count for fifteen seconds. Multiply that number by four to see how many times your heart beats in a minute. To take the pulse at the wrist, turn the palm up and place the other palm around the back of the hand, wrapping the three fingers around the wrist. Follow the same procedure used for the throat.

A low resting heart rate is healthier than a high one because it means your heart is strong and efficient and pumps more blood with each beat than a less conditioned heart does. The speed at which a heart beats varies from person to person and depends on one's size, shape, and amount of exercise. For a large male endurance athlete a resting pulse rate should be between 36 and 60. For a female endurance athlete it should range from less than 40 up to 70. A woman's resting pulse rate is always higher than a man's because females have smaller hearts, which means that their hearts need to beat more times to do the same load of work as a larger heart. The average resting heart rate for all endurance athletes is between 36 and 70. For the average person who exercises regularly the rate is between 60 and 80, and for the sedentary population it is between 68 and 90.

THE EFFECT OF EXERCISE ON THE BRAIN

Regular exercise is addictive. Repeatedly performing the same physical task creates a gentle, meditative state.

It is my theory that the "high" people feel after prolonged exercise may be due to the release of endorphines (see "What Causes Fatigue?" earlier in this chapter) *or* to low oxygen supply to the brain. Blood and oxygen service the working muscles first and deprive the brain somewhat. Like the mountain climber who feels "higher" the higher he climbs because of oxygen deprivation, so too the athlete feels "higher" the longer and harder he works out. There have been no reports of serious harm incurred because of oxygen debt. But you can pass out if you rob your brain of *too* much oxygen. In other words, *too* much of a healthy "high" may reap negative results.

If you follow it safely and consistently, you will reap both the short- and the long-term benefits from a well-rounded physical exercise program. According to Dan Sikowitz, you should notice some of the short-term benefits after three months of pursuing an exercise regime:

- Increased endurance or aerobic capacity
- Stronger muscles
- Flexibility

Long-term or lifelong benefits should take effect after eight months to a year of regular exercise:

- A healthy cardiovascular system
- A healthy respiratory system
- Overall health and well-being

I think that the best discovery you can make about exercise is that your body gives back at least—and usually more than—what you put in. How many things in life can you say that about?

12

Journey Through Bodily Pain

Now that you know how the body works during exercise you're ready to take a journey through bodily pain, to learn some of the things that can go *wrong* inside your body while you exercise and what you can do to prevent undue strain or injury.

More often than not, you can avoid hurting yourself if you are aware of why and how injuries occur. Your body usually gives you warnings that all is not well. Listening to them can save you from injury.

What are the warning signals like? What can happen if you don't heed the warning? What are some simple rules for treating an injury? What accidents are unavoidable? What do you do if an accident occurs?

158

Preventable Injuries

BLISTERS

Blisters are a perfect example of an annoyance that can be avoided *by paying attention to your body*—in this case, to your skin. Blisters are caused by friction, by something rubbing against and irritating the skin. Common spots for blisters are the heel and toes, the thumb, and the palm of the hand. Although they are not serious, blisters can be very uncomfortable. If ignored, they can tear open and may become infected. They can also interfere with tomorrow's scheduled workout. They are best avoided.

Sometimes they occur when you increase your workout time dramatically and your skin doesn't have time to build up callous, tough skin it needs for protection. Other times blisters are caused by ill-fitted shoes and socks. Shoes that are too big or small create blisters, as do too-thick socks.

Prevention

To prevent blisters forming on the feet, some athletes rub petroleum jelly into the skin before running. This makes the skin lubricated and soft, less likely to be roughened up by the friction of the shoe rubbing against the skin.

Treatment

Treating a blister is simple. First, clean it off with some rubbing alcohol. Then sterilize a needle and gently puncture the blister, letting all of the fluid drain out. (Don't tear off the top of the blister.) Apply some antibiotic ointment or hydrogen peroxide and bandage to prevent infection.

CHAFING

Chafing is another skin irritation problem created by friction between clothing and skin or skin and skin. Sweat and salt water aggravate chafing. The underarms and groin are common areas for chafing to occur during land activities. In swimming, the back of the neck may be chafed from the bathing cap rubbing against it. For male long-distance swimmers even a clean-shaven face may grow enough stubble over a five-to-ten-hour swim to chafe a swimmer's shoulder raw as his chin brushes it when he breathes.

Prevention

To prevent chafing, rub petroleum jelly into potential irritation areas and/or wear looser-fitting clothing.

Treatment

Rub petroleum jelly into the area to soothe and to help it heal.

STRAINS

Strains are not to be confused with sprains. There is a big difference between the two. You *strain* a muscle or tendon (the fibers that attach the muscle to the bone); you *sprain* a ligament (the tough fibrous bands that hold the bones together when a joint moves). (See "Sprains" later in this chapter.) Strains are not as severe as sprains and *can be prevented*.

A strain is exactly what it sounds like: A muscle or tendon is under pressure and is being forced to overstretch itself. The muscle or tendon then tightens and is painful when pulled or stretched.

A pulled or torn muscle is a kind of strain. Imagine a

cork popping. As it is pulled, the cork lifts off from its tightly fitted spot. It feels the same way inside the body. More tension is applied to the muscle than it can bear and the muscle pulls away from its secure resting spot. You feel a sudden, localized, persistent pain in the muscle. Swimmers are more susceptible to muscle pulls or tears in the shoulder; runners, in the hamstring, quadricep, or calf; cyclists, in the hamstring or quadricep.

To differentiate between different kinds of strains, the Athletic Trainers Association and the American Medical Association have devised a system for measuring the severity of sports injuries. For example, a pulled muscle is a first-degree or mild strain; there is partial or microscopic tearing or stretching of the fibers. A torn muscle is more severe and is termed a second-degree strain. In this injury there is some tearing of the fibers. The most severe of the three injuries, the third-degree strain, occurs when the fibers of a ruptured muscle have been completely severed.

Prevention

To prevent a strain, make sure your muscles are flexible and supple before you work them. Warm-up exercises will get your blood flowing to the working muscles and raise their temperature. They'll be better able to bend and stretch. Dr. Murray Weisenfeld, podiatrist and sports medicine specialist in New York City, believes that half of all the injuries he treats could be avoided by proper stretching and warm-up prior to exercise.

Treatment

If your strain is mild, keep off it, give it rest, elevate, and apply ice. If the muscle problem persists, you should see a doctor.

The severity of the injury determines how long it will take to heal. A first-degree or mild strain could take between three and five days to heal and allow the athlete to return to full activity. A second-degree strain could take between ten and fourteen days to heal. A third-degree strain could take between three and eight weeks or maybe longer to heal and might require surgery.

When you are able to resume your workouts, begin by slowly stretching your muscles. A muscle heals itself by shortening, so it will feel tight. Gradually increase the length and difficulty of the workout.

Shin Splints

Shin splints have been classified as muscle strains, but doctors believe they are caused by the inflammation of the semitransparent, thin membrane covering the shinbone (periosteum). Picture the shin as a piece of chicken leg bone with a cellophane-type covering encasing the bone. A shin splint is caused when the bone covering is pulled away from the bone.

According to John Howard, shin splints cause a sustained painful, burning feeling. "You actually feel the separation. . . . Imagine having those things ripped apart. That's what it feels like." For John it creates sharp pain on every step.

Prevention

The best protection against shin splints is to understand why they occur and to try to eliminate the poor running habits that cause them. Unfortunately, though, the real warning for shin splints is a slight amount of achy pain in the lower front or side leg muscle. And once you feel that pain, you've already got shin splints. Dr. Weisenfeld suggests that runners use that warning as a chance to get rid of the condition before it gets worse. "A little bit of pain is an early warning," explains Dr. Weisenfeld. "But pain is progressive. It's time to find the problem, to stop it before it becomes a serious problem."

There are two areas of the leg that are affected by shin splints: the front (anterior) and the inward side of the leg (posterior tibial). The front shin splints can be avoided by eliminating poor running habits, such as leaning forward instead of keeping the torso erect while moving, warming up properly and thoroughly, not doing hills or speed work until your muscles are in shape and can handle the increased work, landing heel to toe and not the reverse, making sure your shoes fit properly and are not too big.

Posterior tibial shin splints affect the inner side of the leg and are not avoidable for everyone because they are caused by your foot's structure. Runners who have collapsed or weak arches and whose feet pronate (turn inward) are bound to have symptoms of shin splints. (People whose feet supinate—turn outward—will not.) This is because the main support of the arch is the calf muscle. When the arch collapses, it pulls on the side leg muscle and strains it.

Treatment

The treatment for shin splints is to cut down on your running or try other sports like swimming. The less you run, the better your shins will feel. You might even feel as though the shin splints have gone away for good. But they haven't. To prevent them or to decrease the pain when you run again, reduce inflammation of the shin area by icing it before and after you run. If the pain persists or increases, see a doctor. Very painful shin splints could actually be stress fractures of the shinbone. You'll need an X ray to check for this. It could be helpful to see a podiatrist, who might recommend arch supports, orthotics, or shoes specially designed for pronators (people whose arches are low and whose feet roll inward excessively).

Stress Fractures

Stress fractures are small cracks in the surface of the bone caused by undue pressure. They can occur suddenly or gradually as a result of overuse. They occur frequently in the long thin metatarsals, bones that attach to your toes. Stress fractures are also common on the lower leg—along the shin, three inches above the ankle to three inches below the knee.

Stress fractures are painful. The pain is in a narrow area. When you touch it, it hurts. John Howard had stress fractures of the foot. "It was serious enough so that any pressure, any load created by running, would immediately cause excruciating pain," recalls John, who has a high instep. People with high arches are especially prone to stress fractures because when they land they don't distribute the force of the impact throughout the leg. Instead, their feet absorb too much of the pressure.

Prevention

Stress fractures are difficult to prevent. If you have high arches, pay special attention to the way your foot lands. Be aware of overuse or increased pressure on the feet.

Treatment

This is not an injury that you should treat yourself. To confirm that the injury is a stress fracture, two X rays are usually taken. When the injury first occurs or is noticed, it is sometimes too small to be picked up by an X ray. After two or three weeks, a stress fracture can be picked up by a second X ray because scar tissue will have formed over the crack. Dr. Weisenfeld advises patients suffering from stress fractures to stop running and to switch to a sport that won't extend the injury.

TENDONITIS

Tendonitis is a strain of a tendon. Although it might occur in any athlete, the injury is most noticeable in individuals who exercise regularly and in the muscles they use and need most. (A weekend tennis player, for example, who contracts a mild form of tendonitis—tennis elbow—might not play for another week and thus may give the injury a chance to heal.)

In swimmers, tendonitis usually occurs in the shoulder. Among runners and cyclists, the problem is called Achilles tendonitis, located in the tendon that connects the heel to the calf muscle. Tendons don't stretch very much on their own. If the calf muscle is tight, it will stretch the tendon, causing inflammation and resulting in a dull, burning pain as the tendon rubs against its encasement or sheath. Stretching and working at lengthening the calf muscle can eliminate the chances of the injury occurring.

Prevention

Tendonitis is an injury caused by an imbalance in stroke or running form. One early warning might be a dull burning sensation in the joint. If this occurs, ice the area after each workout for no longer than twenty minutes.

Treatment

Most doctors recommend a complete layoff while the inflammation subsides. If it's a mild case, you can work through it. I've been swimming with slight tendonitis for over two years. The pain is no more than occasional aching and does not get worse.

In some cases when athletes choose to work through the injury, it just goes away. Other times the pain lessens, but the inflammation gets worse. There's no clear-cut cure. You've got to play it by ear. The best treatment is to ice the area and to cut back on exercising the area. Most important, try to correct the imbalance or the weakness that caused the injury in the first place so that it will not recur.

Torn Cartilage

Torn cartilage does not fit into a clear-cut category. Cartilage is a gristlelike material which lines the tips of the bones in a joint; it has no blood vessels or nerves running through it. Its chief function is to absorb shock in the joint. When a piece of cartilage is torn, the end of the bone is unprotected and can be worn down by rubbing against the cartilage of nearby bones.

Prevention

In some cases a torn cartilage is an overuse injury. At other times it is a side complication which occurs when a ligament tear also damages the cartilage. The injury that befell Jenifer Levin, a novelist, during the 1984 New York City Marathon was torn knee cartilage. "First there was a shooting pain. Then it felt as though pieces of glass were rolling and rattling around and were cutting into the bottom and sides of my knee. I hobbled for about ten miles and then stopped at sixteen miles." Jenifer was told that her injury was caused by overuse, but doctors don't understand exactly how or why this injury happens. Muscle balance or weakness in the quadriceps or knee could result in injury to the cartilage, but, unfortunately, a main characteristic of a

166

cartilage injury is that you don't know you've got a problem of imbalance until it's too late and you're injured.

Treatment

A torn cartilage is unlike most injuries because it doesn't heal by itself. Often, orthoscopic surgery is required in which three pinhole-size incisions are made in the knee and the cartilage is shaved similar to the way a splinter on a piece of wood is sanded down. This is done to protect the piece of bone exposed by the space where the cartilage is broken or chipped.

If the injury is mild, some people choose to live with the pain. They're taking a chance. A slight tear or crack in the knee's cartilage, for example, may cause the knee to lock. "It is the cause of what is known as the trick knee. Once it's torn, it's torn," says Bob Reese, athletic trainer for the New York Jets. "It can cause locking or it can cause the knee to give out." Victims of torn cartilage can continue to work out and tolerate the pain, or take up a sport which doesn't stress the knee.

CRAMPS

Muscle cramps are a result of mild dehydration and the loss of a certain amount of vitamins and minerals such as sodium, chloride, and potassium. Any muscle can cramp up. What is happening is that all the fibers within the muscle are contracting involuntarily, and this causes a localized, acute pain.

According to Reese, cramps are treated as mild strains. "Even though the person may be fine and experience some achiness, if we don't pay attention and treat it aggressively, they end up getting a true first-degree strain because the cramp does cause weakness. . . . We feel that there is some muscle damage when you have a severe cramp and it should be treated accordingly."

Prevention

To prevent cramps, athletes are encouraged to take in great quantities of liquid. A controversy lies, however, in what kinds of liquids to take in: water or electrolyte drinks (like Gatorade), so named because they contain sodium, potassium, and chlorine in the form of electrically charged particles (ions). Some sports experts and coaches maintain that the body needs to replace not only the liquid but also the minerals lost through sweat. Says Reese, "We seem to be finding that the best way to approach cramps is to make sure athletes are well hydrated with electrolyte solutions prior to the bout of exercise or competition, even days before it. For example, suppose we're going down to Miami in late December and it's been twenty degrees up here and we're going to be out in seventy-degree weather. My guys don't feel thirsty out here. But we make them force their fluids and make them take Gatorade home at night to sip on the week before."

Other sports physiologists claim that you get all the minerals you need in a well-balanced diet and that large quantities of *water* are needed and are most useful to the body *a few days before* a race or game. Dan Sikowitz recommends drinking eight ounces of water an hour two or three days prior to a race. "During a competition, it's the liquid you need," he says. "You usually pass all the electrolytes out of your system anyway, and their presence can slow down the absorption of the liquid in the stomach."

Whether you choose to stay hydrated with electrolyte drinks or with water, remember to drink as much as you can several days *prior* to an event or race. *During* an event, *drink before you are thirsty,* at least three times an hour.

You're losing a lot of fluid, whether you realize it or not. If you wait until you are thirsty, it's already too late—you're more dehydrated than you should be.

Treatment

If you get a mild cramp during exercise, *don't panic*. Fear and tension make it feel worse. Cramps do not drown swimmers; panic does. *Don't stop.* That makes the muscle contract more. *Keep going* as you concentrate on loosening and relaxing the cramped muscle. Picking up your pace may actually help.

HEAT EXHAUSTION

Heat exhaustion is also caused by dehydration. An athlete suffering from it will feel weak, exhausted, and dizzy and can sometimes become unconscious. Body temperature will be normal or slightly higher than normal, and although the athlete's cooling system is working properly and he is sweating profusely, dehydration is the culprit. The athlete has lost so much body fluid that there is also a decrease in blood volume because he is sweating more than usual. Some sports medicine experts claim that this was the ailment that plagued Gabriela Andersen-Schiess at the end of her 1984 Olympic marathon run when she staggered into the stadium and awkwardly limped around the track. One of the reasons she wasn't pulled off the track might have been that the doctors observed she *was sweating*. Her cooling system was functioning, and heat exhaustion is not considered as dangerous as other heat ailments—namely, heatstroke. (See below.)

John Howard describes dehydration and heat exhaustion:

I was doing the Race Across AMerica, a ten-day blitz, and I totally bombed out on the first day in the Mojave Desert. It was 115°. I didn't feel thirsty, which was probably the first mistake. So I didn't drink, didn't drink. Then I went into a very serious state of dehydration where all my muscles, every muscle I had been using, cramped. I just physically collapsed and passed out in the desert. What I did was just sleep it off. Woke up feeling refreshed and got back on my bike, continued racing. But it cost me the race.

I don't know why I wasn't thirsty. That's just the way the body is, it doesn't always tell you these things. You have to know for yourself. From then on, I drank, but by then the worst of it was over.

Prevention

The obvious way to prevent dehydration and heat exhaustion? Drink, drink, drink. The slogan of the road is drink *before* you are thirsty.

Treatment

Drink and cool down as soon as possible. If symptoms or weakness persist, see your doctor immediately.

HEATSTROKE

Heatstroke is the most dangerous result of dehydration. It occurs suddenly. The athlete is already dehydrated. He is hyperthermic, which means that his body temperature has *risen* dramatically. His temperature has risen so high that the body's cooling system is unable to function. He *stops* sweating and his skin becomes dry—which is how you know it's heatstroke and not heat exhaustion. Some athletes have collapsed into unconsciousness.

Prevention

To prevent heatstroke, follow the same advice as for the other heat ailments and drink, drink, drink.

Treatment

Seek medical help at once. Meanwhile, it's important to lower the victim's temperature immediately, using ice packs, iced towels, or a cold bath. A temperature over 106° for more than a few minutes can result in permanent damage to the brain, liver, or kidney cells.

Hypothermia

The opposite of hyperthermia is hypothermia, which is a dramatic drop in body temperature. It happens most often to long-distance swimmers exercising in water temperatures below 70°. Hypothermia is very dangerous. The body's core temperature drops and slows down all the body's functions: The heart slows, the brain doesn't receive enough oxygen. Everything cools down. It feels like you're going to sleep.

As the brain and heart go to sleep, the swimmer feels no pain, only a calm, dazed sensation. He has stopped shivering. He appears gray, his lips are ashen. He is in big trouble. He may respond dully to questions from his crew or not be able to respond at all.

Below, the father of an English Channel swimmer tells the story of his son's battle with hypothermia on a particularly rough, cold day in the English Channel.

My son battled rain and waves for over twelve hours. When his body core temperature began dropping irreversibly, he began to swim away from the escort boat. Then he swam in circles. He couldn't answer my questions. He didn't know his name. He swam around the boat a couple of times and began passing dangerously close to the ship's propeller.

I kept watching, wanting our dream of crossing the English Channel to come true. As long as he could swim, I thought I could direct him toward France. But after he crossed behind the propeller a second time, it was time to pull him out. The boy had lost his ability to reason and would surely have lost a limb in the propeller if we didn't stop him.

It was a difficult task getting a big, strong, greasy, unwilling swimmer into the little dinghy tied to the main escort boat. Eventually we succeeded. When he was safely out of the water and on the dinghy, he clutched the sides, in a daze, not moving. I had to pry his fingers from the side because four-foot waves were smashing us against the sides of the mother ship. It was a small miracle that his fingers and hands were not broken.

As his core temperature began to return to normal with warm blankets and warm liquids, he realized that he wasn't swimming anymore. He screamed obscenities at me for stopping him.

The next morning when I told the story at breakfast, he didn't remember *any* of it. I knew we made the right choice. He could have died if we hadn't stopped him.

Prevention

You should swim with an escort or with someone else. Hypothermia is especially dangerous because the cold causes the athlete's body to shut down and could cause delirium. The athlete's temperature can go so low that he or she can no longer make a rational decision, which is why the swimmer needs a coach or trainer to make the decision to pull him out of the water.

Acclimatize gradually to cold water by training in it for

increasingly longer stretches of time. Try gaining some extra body fat (weight) to help insulate you.

Drink hot liquids regularly during a cold-water swim.

Treatment

Wrap in warm blankets or towels. Provide hot fluids and massage skin to get blood circulating. Victims of hypothermia are usually hospitalized immediately so professionals can get their temperature back up to normal.

Unavoidable Injuries

These are injuries that can't be prevented. They happen unexpectedly because of an accident, a fall, or a sudden blow. There is nothing you can do to prevent them, except perhaps to concentrate intensely, keep your eyes on the road, and spot obstacles *before* they stop you.

SPRAINS

A sprain is a severe strain to a ligament and takes longer to heal than an ordinary strain. The ligament is a strong fibrous band that surrounds the joints and attaches bone to bone. Ligaments themselves cannot be strengthened. They can, however, be protected by strong muscles supporting the joints.

Twisting your ankle as you trip over a curb, pothole, or other obstacle may result in a sprain. As the joint twists, it stretches or tears the ligament. It usually moves back in by itself, but sometimes needs help. In any case it causes sharp pain and swelling. I recall when I severed the anterior cruciate ligament in my left knee. There was a distinct ripping sound and a wrenching feeling as the joint popped out of place and tore the ligament. The pain was sharp, specific, and intense. Swelling started pretty fast.

As with strains, there are varying degrees of severity in sprains. A mild injury or first-degree sprain is a microscopic tear in the ligament. A second-degree injury is a tear, and a third-degree is a completely severed ligament.

Ankle sprains are the most common for runners. For some an ankle sprain can become a chronic problem. The ligament and joints become so loose that the injury recurs.

The knee is also high on the list for joints easily sprained. But any joint can be sprained by tripping, falling on it, or receiving a heavy blow.

Treatment

A sprain should be acknowledged and treated immediately. Some runners might be determined to finish the run after the incident occurs. But they should *not* continue. According to Dr. Weisenfeld, the first twenty-four hours is the crucial time to care for a sprain. Stop immediately. Elevate the leg and ice the area. It may turn black and blue from internal bleeding. Have it looked at by a doctor. It will need to be kept immobilized for a while.

How long a sprain takes to heal depends on its severity. A first-degree sprain can take between four and six weeks to heal, a second-degree may take six to eight weeks. Some third-degree injuries require surgery and a cast and can take anywhere from four to eight weeks to heal.

DISLOCATIONS

Shoulders, kneecaps, and fingers are the joints that most often become dislocated. The injury occurs when the joint is forced out of place as a result of a bad fall or being hit by someone or something. There are two kinds of dislocations: One occurs when the joint is completely displaced. It moves out of its socket and stays out. The other is a partial dislocation called subluxation. Here the joint pops out and then slides back in immediately on its own.

According to Jets trainer Bob Reese, dislocation occurs most frequently in adolescents because their ligaments are loose and don't begin to tighten up until they are in their mid-twenties. "As you get older, there is more tendency to tear or rupture a ligament than to stretch it," explains Reese. "You are also more liable to break a bone because the bones get weaker while the ligaments get stiffer and tighter. As an adolescent, the bones are still growing and are pretty pliable so you don't have as many broken bones; you get dislocations."

Dislocations or subluxations can also happen to people who are loose-jointed. Doctors can perform a series of tests to determine whether your joints are loose or tight. People who have loose joints (sometimes they're referred to as being double-jointed) have joints which permit a great range of movement. Sally Friedman, an artist and marathon swimmer, says that she has always been double-jointed and that she dislocated her shoulder while preventing a fall. "I was running down the stairs, tripped, and caught the banister to stop myself from falling. I had this incredible pain in my shoulder, a real sharp pain, but I didn't know what had happened. I only knew my shoulder was out because I felt it go right back in." Over a seven-year period Sally dislocated the same shoulder about six times. Recurrence is not unusual. The joint is susceptible to the injury because the ligaments which hold it in place are too loose to do their job: Once stretched, they don't go back to their original length.

Treatment

See a doctor immediately to have the dislocated joint put back in place. Even if the joint goes right back on its own, you should seek medical help anyway to make sure that you don't have any other injury, and to make sure that you are prepared to handle the injury if it happens again.

A first-time dislocation takes about six weeks to heal. In that time the ligament will have regained some stability. Meanwhile, overall healing of the ligament will continue for about a year. To strengthen and protect the area, ask your doctor to suggest exercises that will build muscles in the tissue surrounding the joint. The only permanent cure is surgery.

BREAKING A BONE

There are many different types of bone fractures or breaks. A broken bone is completely severed. At the time of an accident, it's sometimes difficult to tell whether it's a sprain or a break. Some people say that if you are close to the person you can *hear* the bone break. "It's like breaking a stick in half," says Reese. "Usually the player will hear it as a sound more than he'll feel it. You'll ask them what it felt like and they'll say, 'It kind of crunched, snapped, popped.' "

Spike Steingasser broke his ankle riding a motorcycle in a practice run before a motocross race.

I wasn't going very fast, about fifteen miles an hour. The mud was two feet deep—but I didn't know it *wasn't* mud. When your foot is in soft mud, you can drag it through. But this turned out to be dust, like clay. The momentum of my bike made my foot go backwards. I felt my ankle snap, felt it crack. It hurt, but I finished out the lap. When I got off the bike and tried to stand, I felt a stabbing pain. It made me sick to my stomach.

I've broken other bones before and it feels like stubbing your toe really badly except that the pain doesn't go away. The ankle pain was super sharp,

going up my leg. Mine was called a greenstick fracture. Instead of breaking in half, the bone cracked
along the grain the way a piece of wood cracks up the
middle.

My leg was put in a cast. For the first three or four
days after the break, the bone hurts where the break
is. Then it only aches and then you don't feel pain
anymore.

Treatment

Broken bones need immediate attention. X rays are
taken to determine the severity of the break. Depending on
the severity, the bone will usually be put in a soft or hard
cast. Individuals can usually resume activity after three
weeks to three months, depending on the age of the victim
and the seriousness of the break. The injury shouldn't
recur—or the limb remain vulnerable—if the break has been
properly treated.

HEAD CONCUSSION

A concussion is caused by a sharp blow to the head or by
falling on your head. It may not hurt—and might go unde-
tected—at first, but within forty-eight hours the tissues
inside the skull swell against the skull bone and cause
tremendous pressure. You get a bad, nagging headache at
the place of impact, usually around the forehead or at the
base of the skull. It's not a normal throbbing headache in
the temples or in the sinuses. This is a nagging feeling as
though your head is swelling inside—which it is.

The victim might also experience a transient loss of
consciousness, memory loss concerning the incident, nausea, or vomiting. Physicians will be on the alert for warning
signs that the injury is severe or might result in complica-

tions. Some of these signs are constant headaches, vomiting or nausea, weakness in an arm or leg, and disorientation.

Treatment

Any blow to the head should be checked by a physician, who can then determine the severity of the injury and its proper treatment.

If the injury is mild, rest is the main treatment. Some doctors may recommend aspirin substitutes which won't interfere with swelling or bleeding the way aspirin does. (Aspirin stops swelling and thins the blood.) In cases where there is worry about the extent of the injury (especially with young children), concussion victims are frequently awakened from sleep to make sure that they have not lost consciousness.

Some accidents are impossible to avoid. Hidden potholes, inadvertent collision with a teammate or competitor, a deer dashing across your path—all are difficult to see, hear, or sense coming. The best you can do is listen carefully to your body and pay attention to your surroundings.

Always concentrate on what you're doing. Sometimes, unconsciously or subconsciously, you get into an accident because you don't want to be out there and need an irrefutable excuse to quit. Watch where you are going and listen for foreign sounds which signal the approach of dangerous live or inanimate objects. You can prevent most injuries by *being alert* and by *taking responsibility* for your actions.

Finally, realize that *pain is your body's way of communicating. It's telling you that something is wrong and that you'd better pay attention. Learn to listen.*

13

Common Questions and Unorthodox Answers About Endurance Sports

Diet Questions

How long should you wait to swim after you have eaten?

I jump right in. I eat *while* I swim. The longer the workout, the more I eat beforehand. I've eaten eggs, French toast, juice, rolls, cheese, and more before a morning workout. I've swum through the night after a dinner of pasta in butter.

When working out with food in your stomach, it may not be as comfortable as you would like because the blood needed for digestion is being pumped to the working muscles. Your body may feel a little confused, but it won't hurt you.

179

I don't recommend eating full-course meals just before a run, a hard sprint set, or a tough workout, but I do believe you should eat enough to get you through your workout.

Do you diet?

No. To "diet," by definition, means to *limit* or *regulate* what you eat and how much. I eat as much of the foods as my body needs in order to be healthy. I trust my body implicitly. It tells me when, how much, and what to eat. I listen carefully and we get along very well.

I honestly believe that "dieting" is the leading cause of weight problems. The only time I had a yo-yo weight problem was as a teenager—when I was *constantly* on diets.

No one plan, person, or book can dictate to you what *your* body needs in order to be healthy. Your dietary needs are different from mine and from those of the person sitting next to you. Your body's needs change from day to day, season to season, depending on the demands you place on it, the weather, your health.

Any diet that tells you how *much* and exactly *what* to eat *cannot* work in the long run. Any diet that eliminates or highly restricts an entire food group will, in time, deprive you of essential nutrients and can be dangerous. You may lose weight by dieting—for a month or a year. But "dieting" will *not* keep weight off for life.

The only way to keep weight off is to exercise and to learn to trust your body to tell you what it needs for health. The problem is that most people have muted their body's natural voice with bad eating habits over the years. For them it may be difficult to find their body's natural balance. But it can be done.

I recommend going through your refrigerator and cupboards and throwing away anything containing refined sugars and white flours, chemicals, and additives. The shelves might look rather bare when you're done. Next time you go grocery shopping, read labels and buy only *whole* foods. You'll find that most things frozen, canned, or packaged will have additives and chemicals and that the only things you'll be putting into your shopping cart are fresh foods.

I did it several years ago—purging my kitchen, that is. I was amazed at how quickly my craving for junk food and sugars (even my beloved Chunky bars) disappeared as my body got cleaner and healthier. In time, your body won't tolerate what you used to inflict on it as a matter of habit.

If you eat healthfully and intelligently, you should never need to go on "diets."

How do you determine a "healthy" weight?

This is a question that has plagued weight-conscious people for years. They read ideal-weight charts and books on weight loss. While looking at magazine pictures, they fall in love with a fantasy weight. It is rarely based on health.

A healthy weight is one that is naturally maintained. With proper exercise and a well-balanced, nonjunk diet, the body's weight seems to level off by itself. It may fluctuate by a pound or two, going up by as much as five to ten in the winter, or going up as you get older and your metabolism slows down.

I know I am too thin when I get sick often or when my energy level falls off sharply. I know I am too heavy when I feel bloated, sluggish, and inactive. I know I am at a healthy weight, regardless of what the scale may say, when I feel good, strong, and have a high energy level.

Do you take vitamins?

Sometimes. When I am under stress, before a long workout, or when illness threatens to invade, I take vitamins C, E, and a multivitamin. But I believe that if you eat a wide variety of healthful foods and are not placing unusual demands on your body, you don't need to spend a lot of money on vitamins that you will simply eliminate through your urine.

What do you eat during an event?

I eat to restore glucose (blood sugar), which is my main energy supply. The idea behind eating during an endurance event is to replace the calories which are being burned up—and there are a lot of them. In many cases, such as a marathon swim or an Ironman triathlon, you must eat throughout the event.

I always choose foods that are easy for my stomach to break down. To keep me warm during a swim, I drink water, hot chocolate, or tea with milk or honey. In a hot-weather triathlon I'll take in a lot of Gatorade, diluted juices, water, and/or bananas. I know some athletes who eat outrageous things during an event—whole-wheat sandwiches with bananas, honey, and crushed granola bars; sausage; or pizza. Nutrition experts would cringe, but the bottom line is: Do what works best for you. The only way to find out is to experiment with different foods.

How do you eat during an event?

While running, you are offered water, Gatorade, or fruit at regular intervals along the route. When you're bicycling, you drink from your water bottle at regular intervals and carry fruit with you.

During a long-distance swim it's a little trickier. An escort boat always accompanies you, and a friend or trainer on board is there to feed you. I eat while treading water. Liquids are the most popular nourishment and can be passed in a Styrofoam cup. I prefer a bicycle water bottle attached to a string. That way, water doesn't splash into my drink and I can get a good feed no matter how rough the seas are. When I'm through, my trainer can pull the bottle up by the string and I don't have to waste time trying to hand it back. Solid food such as a sandwich or piece of fruit is passed by hand or placed in a colander, attached to a broomstick, which is extended out over the water. I feed once every thirty or sixty minutes. I know some swimmers who feed more often.

Training Questions

Is there a minimum *amount of time required to work out, when less isn't really doing any good?*

Yes. I think you must do at least twenty minutes of sustained activity to be getting any benefit from the exercise. After twenty minutes I'm not exactly sure what it is that happens, but something "clicks" over. You've worked through the waste in your system, the mental blocks, you've gotten past the point where you want to quit. You've broken a sweat and your pulse is up. You are getting something out of the work you put in. And you *begin* to feel good—really good.

When you first start working out, you may not be able to do twenty minutes. You'll need to build up to it. But shoot for twenty minutes as your *minimum* exercise time.

Do you stretch before exercising?

It depends on the workout and how long it will last. I used to do a complete stretching routine before short workouts, but as I began increasing my distance, my body was so well tuned from its last workout that I didn't have to stretch.

The point of any warm-up exercise is to get your body ready to work. Flexible, warmed-up muscles are less prone to injury.

Choose the kind of warm-up that works best for you. It doesn't matter what you do as long as you do something. I think the best way to warm up for swimming, running, or biking is to do the activity itself—very slowly. Walk before you run, or jog slowly in place. Bike on level ground before you hit the hills. Backstroke gently before sprinting hard. The same goes for lifting weights: Slowly run, bike, swim, or gently stretch to warm up and loosen your muscles.

If you do stretch, do it right. Hard, jolting bounces are no good; they can pull or tear ligaments or muscles. Make your stretches a smooth, extended reach.

I want to strengthen my abdominals, tone up my legs, and develop some muscle definition in my arms. What exercises should I do?

Each endurance sport builds a different kind of body. Biking emphasizes quadriceps, running concentrates on calves and hamstrings. Neither does much for the upper body. Swimming works every muscle in the body, including the stomach, if you reach and pull hard enough.

You can complement your sport with Nautilus exercises, which improve strength and flexibility. Each machine concentrates on sculpting a specific body part and developing muscle definition.

Common Questions and Unorthodox Answers

The best way to build the body you want is to take an honest look at yourself, decide what area you want to improve, and choose a well-rounded exercise program. Combine your favorite sport with some specific weight machines—toss in bent-knee sit-ups for the abdominals— and after thirty minutes a day, four or five days a week, you'll see improvement in as little as six weeks.

Do you wear sweat clothes while working out in the gym?

No. I wear the most loose-fitting, comfortable, highly ventilated clothing I can find. When I get out of the water, off my bike, or finish my run, I put sweats on to keep my warm muscles from cramping or getting cold and tight.

I do not understand why anyone wears sweat clothes while working out in the gym. My guess is they think that the more they sweat, the more weight they'll lose. They're wrong. They are losing only *water weight—not* pounds of fat—and they are taking a serious chance on overheating.

When you work out hard, you sweat and need to replace the liquids you lose. Be sure to drink fluids before, during, and after exercise. If you don't replenish those fluids, you risk dehydration.

What is the best time of day to work out?

Each of us has his or her own personal body clock. Some are "night" people, others are "morning" people. As an endurance athlete who puts in two, three, sometimes four, training sessions in a day, I cannot afford the luxury of choosing a best time of day to work out. My body must be able to perform at any hour, on any amount of sleep.

We woke to prepare for my swim across the English

Channel at 2:00 A.M., so I got only about three hours of sleep before my eighteen-hour swim. My double swim around Manhattan began at 10:30 P.M. and lasted for twenty-one hours. I had been awake for about eight hours before I began. Athletes like Stu Mittleman and John Howard have run or biked around the clock several days in a row. Training must be geared toward performing whenever the tide calls. I have to ignore my body clock on occasion.

For the person who is looking for the ideal thirty or sixty minutes to work out, it is best to experiment. If you find your morning run has left you bleary-eyed and incoherent, try running after work. It may be just what you need to relax. Or maybe your evening swim is too easy to talk yourself out of after a long day at the office. Try starting off the morning with a pleasant, cool, eye-opening swim. It may carry you through the day and make work easier.

No one can tell you exactly when to work out or for how long. You need to find that out for yourself.

Are you ever too old to begin exercising or to increase your endurance?

No! I have a friend who began running marathons after he turned forty. Six years later his times are *improving*. Dr. Adrian Kanaar, a seventy-three-year-old man, swam around Manhattan Island in the 1984 swimming race. He is in terrific shape and continues to swim and practice medicine. My father is over sixty and began distance biking (forty or more miles a workout) just a few years ago. He is fitter now and can go farther than he could ten years ago.

No matter when you begin, you will improve fairly steadily for about seven years, then level off. I didn't start swimming long-distance until I was twenty-five and I have only just begun.

Common Questions and Unorthodox Answers

Do you find massage therapy beneficial?

Yes. I have a thorough rubdown from my shiatsu therapist at least once a week when I'm in training. I believe it keeps my injury rate down, loosens up my muscles, and is a luxury I think my body deserves. Massage therapy is an integral part of my training, like adequate sleep and proper eating.

How do you adjust to swimming in the ocean after swimming in a pool?

Swimming in open water is worlds apart from pool swimming. Obviously, there are no lanes or lines on the ocean floor to guide you. For your first few ocean swims, go up or down the coast a few yards from the water's edge. Keep the shore within view and use it to guide you on a straight course.

To swim in a straight direction, work at developing a symmetrical stroke. You'll also need good sighting techniques, so practice lifting your head high enough to see where you are without losing too much time or wasting too much effort. Learn to check your position by focusing on a marker on land or water every twenty-five or thirty strokes. With practice you'll integrate sighting into your stroke and breathing pattern.

Pain Questions

How do I know when I've run far enough?

I set weekly mileage goals for myself in each of my workouts—running, swimming, and biking. I may set out to do a short three-mile running set one day and feel so good I'll run eight. Similarly, I may have a ten-mile set in mind when I start, but if my body begs to stop sooner, I listen. When I'm feeling particularly good and strong, my feet are usually the first to call an end to a workout. I can feel the blisters beginning to form as my feet start to sting. I know if I run a half mile more, I will develop blisters that will keep me from running the next day and maybe even longer. So my feet let me know when I've run enough.

Sometimes I get a stabbing pain just under my rib cage or on my collarbone, usually when I'm running or biking very hard. What should I do about that?

One day I saw someone running on the treadmill stop his run abruptly and pinch himself. When I asked him what he was doing, he explained that when he got a sharp cramp, like the one described above, he believed that if he pinched himself *hard,* it wouldn't hurt so much. I thought that was a silly notion, but if it worked for him, I couldn't argue.

Instead, I recommend *not* trying to divert the pain and certainly *not* to stop running. It is easier and more effective to slow down slightly, so you can catch your breath, concentrate completely on the area that hurts, and think of relaxing that place. As you relax, the cramp should subside. Stopping *suddenly* can create more stress and could possibly hurt you. Cramps of this nature are harmless and need not interfere with your run. You can work right through them. The same is true for cramps in the feet or calves while swimming. More severe cramps are an early sign of dehydration or mineral deficiency. (See "Cramps" in chapter 12.)

Common Questions and Unorthodox Answers

Do you ever hallucinate on a long swim?

Hallucination is a strange and not entirely understood phenomenon. I have never hallucinated on my swims, but I have heard some marvelous stories from people who have. I believe hallucination is a warning signal. The body is flooded with so much pain and so overloaded with physical sensation that the mind has to take a break or it will force you to stop. A long swim, with the cold setting in and fatigue weakening you, often creates a hallucinatory phase. If you are that cold, it could very well be a symptom of oncoming hypothermia and should be recognized as a signal to get warmer somehow—either by swimming faster and/or drinking hot fluids more often or getting out.

There are times when the word "hallucination" is inaccurately used to describe what I call *chosen dissociation*. That is when the physical activity becomes so monotonous or painful that I must go somewhere else in my imagination to escape the discomfort. I let my mind wander deliberately, never losing control of consciousness.

True hallucinations means that you're losing mental awareness and can't continue much farther unless you can come back to reality.

Do you ever get sick?

Yes. Healthy people do get sick. I think it's a good idea. Working out hard is stressful. When you push your limits, you break down muscle fibers *and* your resistance to illness. That's how you build strength. The harder I work, the more I lower my resistance. I get sick once or twice every season and think I'm a lot healthier for it.

When you get sick, it's your body's way of saying,

189

"Hey, I've pushed hard enough, I need a rest." So you give it a rest and it cleans itself out—completely. I always come back stronger and fresher than I was before.

Personal Questions

How does being an endurance athlete affect your sex life?

Being an endurance athlete seems to enhance *every* aspect of my life. When you are in good shape, when you feel healthy and strong, when you feel confident about your appearance, you carry those feelings with you into your personal life.

When I am in serious training, I am rarely too tired for sex. If anything, my drive and sensitivity increase. Working out hard gets all the juices flowing. In addition, good sex can relieve some of the stress created during training.

Sure, like anyone who works hard, there are days when I am too exhausted to think of anything but sleep. Yet, like the executive, I have workouts that feel like I've landed a million-dollar deal and I would love to go dining and dancing with an attractive man to celebrate. There are also workouts that feel like a trip to the dentist or being audited by the IRS. Understandably, I'm not up for socializing on those days.

The only real drawback to being an endurance athlete is finding an unintimidated partner in similar shape. I know marathon swimmers who have performed through the night, beyond the dreams of most mortal men, after a nine-hour cold-water swimming race. It is one of the happy fringe benefits of superior conditioning. Contrary to what your track coach told you in high school, there are athletes who have crossed the English Channel or completed grueling triathlons after nights of passionate sex.

Common Questions and Unorthodox Answers

How do you go to the bathroom during an event?

I get asked that question a lot. The answer is simple—I just go.

During a swim you urinate while swimming. No fuss, no bother. The digestive system isn't receiving enough blood to do much more than urinate.

During biking and running events, it's more difficult. If there are no portable bathrooms along the course, start praying for a convenient bush.

What do you do when you get your period?

I am always amazed by this question. I do what every other woman does—I wear tampons and work out the same as always. I am fortunate not to get cramps—I have heard that exercising regularly cuts down on severe cramps in women who suffer from them. Obviously, I can't postpone a major swim because it's my time of the month, so I have to live with it like anyone else.

Have you ever smoked?

No, I've always respected my body too much. Other people's smoke is offensive to me. I don't know any serious endurance athletes who smoke. I have never understood how some dancers could keep smoking despite rigorous performing.

I know a number of runners who used to smoke, but as they increased their mileage, they were forced to choose between the two. Their bodies would not tolerate both, and I'm pleased to report that they chose running. It felt better.

Do you ever marvel at yourself, thinking, "Hey, I can really do these terrific things"?

I am asked that one often and always feel embarrassed. No. I don't marvel at the things I do, mostly because I look at the people who are running six-day races, biking across the country averaging 350 miles a day for ten days straight, or swimming for fifty-four hours in the Gulf Stream. I marvel at what *they* do. In comparison, what I've done seems slight.

When I was acting, I never took comfort in being better than some actors. I needed merely to look at the Oliviers and Hepburns to know what real greatness was and to get honest perspective on my talents.

Sometimes I feel good about what I've done in comparison with what I had done before. I see how I've improved myself and I enjoy that feeling. It is all a matter of getting perspective.

Are there any drawbacks to endurance sports?

The biggest, and perhaps only, drawback for the ultra-athletes is that these sports—by their very nature—require a lot of time. For all the benefit they provide, they are not practical for a person with another full-time career. It means sacrificing.

For the fitness enthusiast who is not hunting for five hours in the day to devote to training for a six-day race, the thirty to sixty minutes you need per day to enhance your life are easily found. The minutes are well worth the extra martini you must skip at lunch, the fortieth round of Trivial Pursuit you will pass up, or the favorite game show you will miss.

192

Common Questions and Unorthodox Answers

Why do you push yourself?

Interviewers and bewildered strangers probe with their questions about my childhood, my personal life, my feelings about myself. They seek some deeply rooted unhappiness or some major dissatisfaction with my life as an explanation for my passion for endurance. They think that something must be missing and that I am searching for it in endurance.

Well, I hate to disappoint them, but I feel good about my childhood and my life, and I don't swim to compensate for lack of love or fulfillment. It may be a factor with some athletes, but I think the real motive is *love*. I love swimming so completely and passionately that I can't seem to get enough sometimes. Swimming, pushing my body in any physical endeavor, makes me feel healthy, strong, happy, vital. I haven't found anything else in life that is that fulfilling and so reliable. I know I feel better inside and out because of swimming and challenging myself. I see no reason to settle for anything less.

Bibliography and Suggested Reading

BOOKS

Averbuch, Gloria. *The Woman Runner*. New York: Simon & Schuster, 1984.

Cooper, Gary L., and Judi Marshall. *Understanding Executive Stress*. Princeton, N. J.: Petrocelli Books, 1977.

Darden, Ellington, Ph.D. *The Nautilus Book*. Chicago, Ill.: Contemporary Books, 1982.

Edwards, Sally. *Triathlon: The Triple Fitness Sport*. Chicago, Ill.: Contemporary Books, 1983.

Howard, John. *The Cyclist's Companion*. Brattleboro, Vt.: The Stephen Greene Press, 1984.

Jerome, John. *Staying with It: On Becoming an Athlete*. New York: Viking Press, 1983.

Levin, Jenifer. *Water Dancer*. New York: Poseidon Press, 1982.

McArdle, William D., Frank Katch, and Victor Katch. *Exercise Physiology: Energy, Nutrition, and Human Performance*. Philadelphia, Pa.: Lea & Febiger, 1981.

Mirkin, Gabe, M.D., and Marshall Hoffman. *The Sports Medicine Book*. Boston: Little, Brown & Co., 1978.

194

Bibliography and Suggested Readings

Newsholme, Eric, and Tony Leech. *The Runner.* Roosevelt, N. J.: Walter L. Meagher.

Nyad, Diana. *Other Shores.* New York: Random House, 1978.

Ornish, Dean, M.D. *Stress, Diet, and Your Heart.* New York: New American Library, 1982.

Selye, Hans, M.D. *The Stress of Life.* New York: McGraw-Hill Book Co., 1976.

Shangold, Mona, M.D., and Gabe Mirkin, M.D. *The Complete Sports Medicine Book for Women.* New York: Simon & Schuster, 1985.

Sharkey, Brian J. *Physiology of Fitness.* Champaign, Ill.: Human Kinetics Publishers, 1979.

Smith, David, with Franklin Russell. *The Healing Journey: The Odyssey of an Uncommon Athlete.* San Francisco, Ca.: Sierra Club Books, 1983.

Weisenfeld, Murray F., and Barbara Burr. *The Runner's Repair Manual.* New York: St. Martin's Press, 1980.

Wennerberg, Conrad. *Wind, Waves, and Sunburn.* New York: A. S. Barnes & Co., 1974.

ARTICLES

Alfano, Peter. "Ultra-Athletes Take It to the Limit." *The New York Times,* June 19, 1983.

Brody, Jane. "Personal Health: Calcium." *The New York Times,* March 6, 1985.

Howard, John. "John Howard." *Ultrasport,* August 1984.

Laurence, Robert P. "Preview: Who Will Win the RAAM?" *Bicycling,* August 1984.

McRae, Michael. "The Longest Ride." *Outside,* February/March 1983.

Mihalik, Maria. "Monitoring Your Heart Rate." *Bicycling,* June 1985.

Morgan, William P. "The Mind of the Marathoner." *Psychology Today,* April 1978.

Murphy, Robert, M.D. "Heat Illness in the Athlete." *The American Journal of Sports Medicine,* vol. 12, no. 4 (1984).

195

Bibliography and Suggested Reading

Newell, Stanley G., D.P.M., and Steven T. Bramwell, M.D. "Overuse Injuries to the Knee in Runners." *The Physician and Sportsmedicine,* vol. 12, no. 3 (March 1984).

"Overtraining of Athletes: A Round Table." *The Physician and Sportsmedicine,* vol. 11, no. 6 (June 1983).

Schimpf, Ann, and Stephanie Lemenowsky. "The Ultramarathon: Can Women Outclass Men?" *Harper's Bazaar,* September 1983.

Williams, Kathy, and Robert L. Shultis. "J. Peter Grace, the President's Chief Cost Cutter." *Management Accounting,* June 1984.

Index

A

Achilles tendonitis, 165
Aden, Vicky, 41, 62, 68, 84
Adenosine triphosphate. *See*
    ATP
Adrenal glands, 137
Adrenaline, 55, 67, 71, 137
Aerobic energy, 141
Aerobic energy pathway, 140
Amenorrhea, 144
Anaerobic energy, 141
Anaerobic threshold, 142
Andersen-Schiess, Gabriela,
    10, 169
Apocrine glands, 149
Asmuth, Paul, 40, 41, 50, 87,
    129, 133
Aspirin, 178

Association, 47
Athletic Trainers Association,
    161
ATP (adenosine triphosphate),
    138–139, 143, 151–152
    regenerating, 139–141
Attentional focuses, types of,
    41–42

B

Baker, Eric, 74
Ball, George L., 61, 104
Bathroom functions, 191
Biking. *See also* Cycling
    and sleep deprivation, 71
    tips for, 121–122
Biofitness Institute, 60, 147

Index

Blisters, 159
  prevention of, 159
  treatment of, 159
Blood pressure, 153–155
Blood sugar, effect of drop in,
  70–71
Body clock, 185
Body fat
  functioning of, 144–146
  as heat insulator, 32, 146,
  173
  ideal amounts of, 145
Bones
  broken, 176–177
  effect of exercise on,
  150–151
  treatment of broken, 177
Brain, effect of exercise on,
  156–157
Breakfast, 109
Breaks, need for taking, 51
Breathing
  as pacing technique, 62
  and swimming, 120–121
Broad focus, 42–43
Brooks, Lyn, 19, 21, 25, 110,
  111
Burnout
  avoiding, 52–62
  causes of, 57–59
  and pacing techniques, 52,
  59–62

C

Calcium, 150
Calipers, 145
Carbohydrates, 34, 108–109,
  137–138, 147
Cardiac system, effect of
  exercise on, 153–155
Cartilage, torn, 166
  prevention of, 166–167
  treatment of, 167

Chafing, 160
  prevention, 160
  treatment of, 160
Channel Swimming Associa-
  tion, 74
Chloride, 167, 168
Chosen dissociation, 189
Coach. *See* Trainer
Complex carbohydrates,
  108–109
Compulsiveness, 53, 58
Concentration
  development of, 40–44
  effect of sleep deprivation
  on, 71
Concussion, 177–178
  treatment of, 178
Councilman, Doc, 30, 31
CP pathway, 139–140
Cramps, 57, 167–168, 188
  prevention of, 168–169
  treatment of, 169
Crashing, 57
Creatine phosphate (CP), 139
Crying, 77–78
Cycling. *See also* Bicycling
  amount of body fat needed,
  146

D

Dawson, Buck, 29, 32
Dehydration, 150, 167, 169–170
Depression. *See* Post-event
  depression
Desire, as motivation, 38
Determination, effect of, on
  endurance, 71–72, 73–75
Diet and dieting. *See* Nutrition
Dinner, 110
Direction, role of, in goal
  achievement, 26–27
Discomfort. *See also* Pain
  using to advantage, 55

Dislocations, 174–175
treatment of, 175–176
Dissociation, 47, 189
Dress rehearsal, and endurance training, 35
Drive, role of, in goal achievement, 26–27

E

Eating. *See* Nutrition
Eccrine glands, 149
Ederle, Gertrude, 13
Electrolyte drinks, 168
Endorphins, 148, 156
Endurance
anticipation of obstacles,
31–33
assessing starting position,
29–30
benefits from, 5–7
challenge of, 3–4
components of, 27–37
discovering your staying
power, 14–15, 63–64
dress rehearsal for, 35
effect of success on, 19–20
goal setting, 28
and lifestyle, 7
mental, 8
mental preparation, 34–35
need for rest and nutrition,
34
phenomenon of, 4–5, 7
physical, 9–10
proving yourself to yourself,
20–21
pushing at own speed, 15–18
putting plan into action, 31
reasons for, 4–5, 193
reassessment of program/
success, 36–37
research of subject, 28–29
role of past experience,
33–34

role of success in, 21–22
seeing goals to completition,
36
setting goals for, 6–7
strategy development, 30
and strength, 4
tapering training to conserve
energy, 35–36
testing your limits for,
13–14, 53
Endurance athlete. *See also*
High-energy endurance
life style; Ultra-athlete
challenge for, 3–4
and goal setting, 5
stereotype of, 39
Endurance sports, drawbacks
to, 192
Energy conservation, and
endurance training,
35–36
Energy-producing system,
functioning of, 141–
143
English Channel
feelings during swim, 66–67,
68, 74–75
preparation for swimming,
30, 31, 32–33
Enzymes, 138
Epinephrine, 137
Essential fats, 144
Exercise. *See also* Training
and consistency, 115
cramps during, 169
effect of
on body, 148–157
on bones, 150–151
on brain, 156–157
on cardiac system,
153–155
on muscles, 143–144
on respiratory system,
151–153
in health clubs, 123–124

Exercise *(cont'd)*
in high-energy endurance life
style, 106–107
and Nautilus equipment,
50–51, 184
setting aside time for,
114–115
tips for, 117–119
Experience, role of, and
endurance training,
33–34
External focus, 42–43

F

Failure. *See also* Finishing;
Quitting
accepting responsibility for
actions, 83–85
admission and acceptance
of, 85–86
importance of finishing,
90–91
learning from mistakes,
82–83
unattained goals, 88–90
use of, as stepping stone,
86–88
viewing in perspective,
81–82
Fatigue, causes of, 146–148
Fats, 108, 137, 147. *See also*
Body fat
Fiber, 108–109
Fight or flight response, 56
Files, Chris, 18, 21
Final kick, effect of, on endurance, 75–76
Finishing. *See also* Failure;
Quitting
and decision not to, 63–65,
72, 80–91
developing mental tough-
ness, 65–66
effect of crying, 77–79

effect of opposition, 77
importance of, 90–91
and positive thinking, 76–77
versus winning, 24–25
Finishing syndrome, 66–76
phase 1—fresh start, 67
phase 2—work, 67–72
phase 3—second wind, 73
phase 4—quiet determina-
tion, 73–75
phase 5—final kick, 75–76
suggestions for getting
through, 76–79
Fitness. *See also* Exercise;
Training
integration of, into life style,
6–7
Focus
development of, 44
shifting of, 43–44
types of, 41–42
use of, 42–43
Focusing, as cause of burnout,
58
Foods. *See* Nutrition
Form, need for proper, 119
Frankfurt, Mike, 19–20, 29, 65,
79, 94–95
Freestyle, 120
Friedman, Sally, 175

G

Gatorade, 168, 182
Glucose, 137–138, 182
Glycogen, 36, 132, 138,
146–147
Goals
and endurance training, 36
evaluation of, 62
and pacing, 47
and post-event depression,
96, 97–99
remembering, and endur-
ance, 39–40

setting, 6, 28, 83
unattained, 88–90
Grace, J. Peter, 104
Greenstick fracture, 176–177

H

Haldeman, Lon, 71–72
Halfway point, effect of, on
    finishing, 69
Hallucinations, 189
Health club workouts. *See also*
    Exercise; Training
tips for, 123–124
Heat exhaustion, 10, 169–170
    prevention of, 170
    treatment of, 170
Heat stroke, 150, 169, 170
    prevention of, 171
    treatment of, 171
High-energy endurance life
    style, 103–111
setting up regimen, 106–111
Hiller, Dr. Doug, 137, 143, 149,
    151–152, 153, 155
Howard, John, 7, 25, 54, 58,
    59, 69, 71, 78, 79, 83,
    84, 88, 95, 96, 111,
    121–122, 162, 164,
    169–170, 186
training for, 126–127
Hydrostatic weighing, 145
Hyperthermia, 170, 171
Hypothermia, 10, 70, 82, 87,
    147, 171–172, 189
    prevention of, 172–173
    treatment of, 173

I

Injuries
    causes of, 53
    occurrence of, 10
    preventable, 159–173
    prevention of, 117, 150, 178

recovery time, 132–134
unavoidable, 173–178
Internal focus, 42–43
Interval training, 129, 141,
    142–143
Ironman triathlon, 7, 84,
    131–132, 182

J

Jacobs, Andrew, 41, 44, 45, 47,
    51, 55, 56, 62
Johnson, P. J., 19, 45, 48, 110
Joints, dislocation of, 174–176

K

Kanaar, Dr. Adrian, 186
Kelly, Rebecca, 49, 58, 61, 76,
    81, 97, 104

L

Lactic acid, 140, 151
Lactate acid pathway, 140
Lactic acid buildup, 147–148
Levin, Jenifer, 166
Lichtman, Steven, 109,
    123–124, 140, 142, 145,
    146, 147
Limits
    initial testing of, 13–14
    testing of, and burnout, 53
Lunch, 109–110

M

Manhattan Double, 37
Marathon, finding proper,
    112–124
Massage therapy, benefits
    from, 187
Menstruation, 191
    and level of body fat, 144
Mental depression, 69

Mental endurance, 8, 34–35
  development of, 65–66
  role of drive and direction
    in, 26–27
  techniques for developing,
    38–51
Mental outlook, 76–77
Mental preparation, and
    endurance training,
    34–35
Mental rehearsal, 45–46
Mental strength, 8
Mental toughness, developing,
    65–66
Mileage, determination of,
    128–129
Mind-set, 64, 76–77
Mistakes, learning from, 82–83
Mitochondria, 138
Mittleman, Stu, 5–6, 44, 57,
    77, 85–86, 88, 97, 106,
    122–123, 186
  training for, 126
Monotony, problem of, 59
Motivation, tips for achieving,
    46–51
Muscle biopsy, 143–144
Muscle cramps, 57, 167–168,
    188
  prevention of, 168–169
  treatment of, 169
Muscles
  effect of exercise on,
    143–144
  weight of, 145
Muscle soreness, and fatigue,
    148

N

Narrow focus, 42–43
Nautilus program, 50–51, 184
Neuromuscular junctions, 146
New York City Marathon,
    23–24

Nicholas, Cindy, 20–21, 29, 30,
    72, 81–82, 88, 94, 96, 98,
    128
Nutrition
  determining healthy weight,
    181–182
  dieting, 180–181
  eating during an event,
    32–33, 182–183
  eating for energy, 32–33,
    107–110
  and endurance training, 34
  and fatigue, 147
  food as energy source,
    137–138
  questions on, 179–183
  for quick energy, 32–33
  and swimming after eating,
    179–180
  vitamins, 182

O

Obstacles
  anticipation of, and endur-
    ance training, 31–33
  and desire to quit, 79
  taking advantage of, and
    motivation, 49–50
Olympics, 20
Orthoscopic surgery, 167
Osteoporosis, 150
Overconfidence, problem of,
    53
Overdoing, symptoms of, 54
Overkicking, 120
Overload principle, 60
Overtraining, 132
  prevention of, 129–130
Oxygen deprivation, 156

P

Pacing
  role of, in motivation, 47

use of, to avoid burnout, 52,
59–62
Pain, 158
coping with, 9–10
cramps as form of, 188
level of, 187–188
positive, 118–119
and preventable injuries,
159–173
questions about, 187–190
as sign of physical limitation,
54–57
and unavoidable injuries,
173–178
using to advantage, 55
warning, 118
Patience, need for, 58
Peaking, 56
Periosteum, 162
Physical endurance, 9–10
Physical exercise. *See* Exercise
Physiological reaction to
stress, 56
Plan, putting into action, and
endurance training, 31
Positive thinking, effect of, on
endurance, 76–77
Post-event depression, 92–99;
See also Success
coping with, 94–98
feeling the loss, 93–94
and setting new goals, 98–99
Potassium, 167, 168
Progressive weight resistance,
60
Pulse
and determining your target
heart rate, 134
method for taking, 155–156

Q

Quitting. *See also* Failure;
Finishing

desire for, and finishing,
68–69
as learning experience, 81
question of, 63–65

R

Race across AMerica, 7, 69,
170
Reagan, Ronald, 104
Reassessment of
program/success, and
endurance training,
36–37
Recovery, 132–134
Reese, Bob, 167, 168, 175, 176
Relaxation, use of as pacing
technique, 62, 119
Research, need for and endur-
ance training, 28–29
Respiratory system, effect of
exercise on, 151–153
Responsibility, accepting for
actions, 83–85
Rest/sleep. *See also* Sleep;
Sleep deprivation
and endurance training, 34
need for, 51, 110–111
Resting heart rate, 135, 156
Ridge, Julie, 75
training for, 127–128
Rivers, Hannah, 17
Routine, breaking up of, 48–49
Runners
amount of body fat needed,
146
Running
tips for, 122–123

S

Sauna suits, 150
Schmidt, Bill, 87, 88
Schmidt, Rob, 87
Schoenberg, Saul, 107

Second wind, effect of, on endurance, 73
Self-esteem, and endurance, 21–22
Sex life, and endurance training, 190
Shin splints, 162
  prevention of, 162–163
  treatment of, 163–164
Sickness, 189–190
Sikowitz, Dan, 60, 147, 157, 168
Simple carbohydrates, 109
Skin-fold method of determining body fat, 145
Sleep. *See also* Rest/sleep; Sleep deprivation
  and hypothermia, 147
  problem of, during long athletic endeavor, 71
Sleep deprivation, 70, 71
  training for, 33
Smith, David, 94
Smoking, 191–192
Sodium, 167, 168
Solomon, Dr. Laurie, 73
Speed, setting own, 15–18
Sports
  choosing, 113–114
  integration of, into life style, 6–7
Sprains, 160, 173–174
  treatment of, 174
Starting position, assessment of, and endurance training, 29–30
Staying power, 63–65
  discovering, 14–15
Steady-state activity, 142
Steingasser, Spike, 176
Strains, 160–161, 173, 174
  prevention of, 161
  treatment of, 161–162
Strategy development and endurance training, 30

Strength, and endurance, 4
Strength training, 133
Stress
  adapting to, 60–61
  common responses to, 56
  negative responses to, 56–57
  symptoms of, and burnout, 53
  using to advantage, 55–57
Stress fractures, 164
  prevention of, 164
  treatment of, 164–165
Storage fat, 144
Stretching, 184
Subcutaneous fat, 144
Subluxation, 175
Success. *See also* Post-event depression
  determining healthiness of drive for, 61
  effect of achieving, 19–20
  types of, 23
Sweat clothes, 185
Sweating, 148–150
Swimming
  amount of body fat needed, 146
  bathroom functions during, 191
  eating during, 32–33, 182–183
  eating prior to, 179–180
  and hallucinations, 189
  and hypothermia, 70, 82, 87, 171–172, 189
  in ocean versus pool, 187
  tips for, 120–121

T

Taper, 35–36
  and post-event depression, 95
Target heart rate (THR), determining, 135

Index

Tendonitis, 165
  prevention of, 165
  treatment of, 165–166
Tennis elbow, 165
Tracking of progress and
  motivation, 48
Trainer, working with, 50–51,
  172, 183
Training. *See also* Exercise
  and age, 186
  amount of time needed for,
    183
  clothes for, 185
  determining mileage,
    128–129
  determining target heart
    rate, 135
  importance of, 38–39
  interval, 129, 141, 142–143
  mental process of, 23–37
  need for warm-up stretching,
    184
  préventing overtraining,
    129–130
  questions on, 183–187
  recovery, 132–134
  strength, 133, 141
  taking the middle road,
    130–131
  time of day for, 185–186
  for ultra-athletes, 125–128
  and undertraining, 131–132
Treadmill, 152
Trial and error, learning by,
  26–27
Trick knee, 167
Twilight hours, 70

U

Ultra-athletes. *See also* Endurance athlete; High-
energy endurance life
  style
  exercise routines of, 106–107
  and mental endurance, 8
  need for patience by, 58
  nutrition for, 107–110
  sleep needs of, 110–111
  training for, 53, 125–135
  use of discomfort by, 55
Undertraining, 131–132
Underwater weighting, 145

V

V02 Max, 152
Visual imagery, 45
Visualization, 45
Vitamins, 182

W

Walkman, need for, 113–114
Warming up, 184
Water weight, 185
Weight, as insulation against
  cold, 32
Weight lifting, 133, 141
Weisenfeld, Dr. Murray, 161,
  162–163, 165, 174
Wind, Waves, and Sunburn, 29
Winning, versus finishing,
  24–25
Winning Edge, 41
Workaholics, 53
Workout. *See* Exercise; Train-
  ing

Z

Zealousness, problem of, 53
Zimmer, Judith, 15–17